NSAI

Best small stories from Aotearoa New Zealand

Edited by Michelle Elvy,
Frankie McMillan
and James Norcliffe

Canterbury University Press

UNIVERSITY OF CANTERBURY
Te Whare Wānanga o Waitaha
CHRISTCHURCH NEW ZEALAND

First published in 2018 by
Canterbury University Press
University of Canterbury
Private Bag 4800, Christchurch
New Zealand
www.canterbury.ac.nz/engage/cup

ISBN 978-1-927145-98-2

A catalogue record for this book is available from the National Library of New Zealand.

Copy editor: Emma Neale
Book design and layout: Aaron Beehre

Printed by Caxton, New Zealand

Published with the support of Creative New Zealand

creative nz
Arts Council of New Zealand Toi Aotearoa

Contents

Essays

14

Preface

Bonsai, the practice of creating miniature trees, is an ancient art.[1] There is something astonishing in the form: a perfect tree, perhaps one thousand times smaller than its full-sized counterpart.

Bonsai, this collection of some of the best small stories from Aotearoa New Zealand, celebrates the art of the compressed narrative form – a short short story trimmed to its essence.

'Flash fiction' is the term most often used for what is arguably the fastest growing literary form worldwide. While 'flash' is a relatively new name, the form has ancient antecedents: the fable, the prose poem, even the joke. In the popularity of the modern form we can see a renaissance of the short short story as practised by writers such as Jorge Luis Borges, Anton Chekhov, O. Henry, Franz Kafka and Gertrude Stein.

The compressed form has deep roots in New Zealand's literature, with its notable history of short story writers, Katherine Mansfield and Frank Sargeson in particular, so it is perhaps not surprising to find such enthusiasm for the very short form here. The New Zealand short short stories anthologies edited by Graeme Lay and Stephen Stratford, with their 500-word limit,[2] were very popular, as is the web journal *Flash Frontier: An Adventure in Short Fiction.* Both *Flash Frontier* and the National Flash Fiction Day (NFFD) competition have seen a rise in the quality and quantity of works submitted since they began in 2012, and the NFFD award events – held on the shortest day of the year in New Zealand's main centres – draw large audiences.

What is it that makes this form so attractive, and why the growing popularity? This book includes essays that set out to suggest some answers to these questions, but here are some thoughts.

One of the paradoxes of creativity is that it often responds well to restraints; for this reason poets may subject themselves to rhyme, to metre or to syllabic pattern. With its arbitrary word limit (300 for this volume, but ranging from 100 to 1000 more generally), flash fiction is a demanding form, but the challenge of

1 The Japanese term *Bon-sai* means 'planted in a container'; the art form derives from an ancient Chinese horticultural practice.

2 The first in this series was *100 NZ Short Short Stories* published in 1997 (Tandem Press).

the constraint is part of the appeal; as one of our contributors remarked, it can be highly addictive. The economy of the form requires precision, and the recognition that what is not said is often as significant as what is.

This is a hugely inclusive and elastic form with protean possibilities: stories may range from the vernacular to the poetic; from the open-eyed to the hyper-subtle; from the comic to the tragic to the deeply ambiguous. Often there is a luminescence to flash fiction. A musicality, too: like poetry, very short stories are best when language-driven. The mood, or moment, is captured quickly – and can remain with you for a long while.

As Joyce Carol Oates has noted, unlike conventional prose which 'generally opens out to dramatise experience and evoke emotion', the short short story is more like poetry, where 'in the smallest, tightest spaces, experience can only be suggested'.[3] In the very short form, the use of imagery invokes a wider world.

All of this makes not only the writing but also the reading of flash intensely satisfying, and we hope that this is the case for readers of this volume.

Which brings us back to the small stories in this book. Many literary journals are forsaking paper for the web, and we saw a great deal of excellent short short fiction by New Zealand writers being published online that we felt deserved to be collected between the covers of a book. We relished the idea of seeking out more of the best work in the genre – both new and previously published, by emerging and established writers – and bringing it all together in one substantial volume.

Bonsai presents a collection of small forms ranging from prose poetry to dialogue-driven story, from lyrical recollections to intimate portrayals. We have also included a number of haibun, a Japanese form incorporating prose and haiku. Like haiku itself, haibun is popular in this country and we can boast a number of accomplished practitioners.

Furthermore, there has been little critical analysis of the short short form in New Zealand, so we wanted to allow space in the book for discussion and exploration of the genre, its complexities and possibilities. The essays included here offer insights from talented exponents of the short short form and will serve as an engaging and useful adjunct to the stories. We hope they will lead to a greater appreciation of this challenging and rewarding form.

---

3 Quoted in Robert Shapard, 'The Remarkable Reinvention of Very Short Fiction' in *World Literature Today*, September 2012; https://www. worldliteraturetoday.org/2012/september/remarkable-reinvention-very-short-fiction-robert-shapard

Acknowledgements

Bonsai has been an exciting project for us and we feel privileged to be part of this pioneering collection of the best New Zealand short short fiction and related forms. We wish to acknowledge the enthusiasm and goodwill of the contributors whose stories and essays feature here; without their generosity this book would not have been possible.

We are grateful to all the writers who sent us new works in response to our call for submissions and we regret that owing to space constraints we were not able to include more.

We would like to thank the writers and publishers of previously published material for allowing their work to be included; details are provided with each story, in grateful acknowledgement, and also to encourage further reading.

We extend special thanks to Tim Jones and Graeme Lay for their assistance; we greatly benefitted from their specialised knowledge, experience and insights.

We are grateful to Emma Neale for her thoughtful copy-editing, and Aaron Beehre for his striking design. Our final thanks must be to publisher Catherine Montgomery and project editor Katrina McCallum at Canterbury University Press for their support and wholehearted commitment to this project.

Michelle Elvy
Frankie McMillan
James Norcliffe
May 2018

ST

OR
IES

Rules

Beneath the spy-holes, laminated rules are pinned on every door. Before leaving, Mere flicks them with her fake feather duster.

No jobs when she left school; this gig came through Karena, her tranny cuz who knew the owner. They shot through to Sydney, left Justin in charge. Thinks he's running the bloody Sheraton.

Perks – like guests – are down. That bypass kicked the town into the long grass. Magpie Mere sifts flotsam and jetsam. *Keep. Chuck. Keep.*

Most days, there's still loose change: her tips. Clothing, sometimes. Even underwear. Gross. Hoodies, T-shirts – okay with a hot wash. No one's gonna miss those. Scored a Diesel denim jacket once. Huge, so aunty Big Becca snaffled that. Toys, she keeps back, in case someone claims them. Then, after a good clean, her Rangi gets the pick; Kidzcentre get the rest. Soft toys are saddest, but Justin won't chase down guests once they've checked out. Reckons you never know their circumstances, like the motel's the scene of some big mystery.

Nowadays, guests keep their I-everythings close as their drugs. No chance. Sometimes there's a necklace caught in the sheets. Cufflinks lurking beneath the bed. Haste makes waste. Fair game.

Her mother's rapt with those pearl studs. Mere held onto them for a month, just in case.

The chunky Rolex from the bedside table glints on her skinny brown wrist. Car-boot? Nah, too obvious. Guests think cleaners nick anything unless it's nailed down. Could be a trap. Anyway, the golden manacle clashes with her primrose rubber gloves. She'll tell Justin – sometimes guests offer rewards. Beats a poke in the eye with a blunt stick. There's rules.

*

Big Becca takes the perks to the massive car-boot round Morrinsville. They split the moolah. Becca guzzles hers. Mere's share goes straight into Rangi's Saver. He won't be no cleaner.

Alex Reece Abbott

A version of this work was published in *To Carry Her Home* (Bath Flash Fiction, Volume One, 2016).

Along the road to the hot rod Beach Hop

Before Romata could playfully hit Jake on the arm, a glossy black 1942 Buick with white-wall tyres sailed past like a moving building. Romata shouted, 'It's time travel seeing that car.'

Jake and Romata in a tangle of adolescent arms, legs and giggling. Jake determined he'd go back in time to rewrite essays, get better marks. Romata said, 'I'll be a billionaire. Buy every 1966 Mustang in existence. But I'll only sell them to cool people.'

Both quiet a while, then Jake said Romata was cool. She smiled, sat with one denim-clad leg draped over his. They simultaneously shouted, '1953, Datsun Delux Sedan, original paint and rare in this country,' as if they'd rehearsed the line. Spent the next three minutes looking at each other, quite lost for words.

*

Mrs Hall from the Ka Pai Fish and Chip shop watched the teenagers outside her place, briefly. Then she tidied sheets of white paper and read a newspaper behind the counter. Couldn't see a word. Just thought about how her husband drove one of those cars, a Buick, when they were young. Able to take yourself anywhere if you could afford the petrol. So simple, the freedom and the way the wind blew inside the car with the windows open. She tossed her hair as if it were again long, glossy, brunette. She smiled and hummed while out the window cars passed by and the teenagers were laughing.

Raewyn Alexander

A version of this work was first broadcast on Radio New Zealand in 2001.

Woodville revisited

It was the first day. Dad resembled a Godfather in his three-piece suit, transitional glasses darkened in the sun. He'd dressed especially, and we spent the day exploring in the hovercraft of an old diesel Mercedes. It seemed to extend the hours, hills crawling by. We paused where green shoulders parted, opening to fresh perspectives of a tartan landscape. Up at the wind farm Dad forgot my name. I remember the reflection of my lost face in his glasses, my cigarette tasting like chlorine. We wrapped our arms around a windmill's throat to feel its heartbeat. Above us, the giant scooped the wind into its long white oesophagus. It took my breath with it too. These days I cross the apostrophe hills to watch my father daydream in an armchair. We are just images moving past his window now. The turbines took all the power that first day, and on the way home we both forgot the milk.

Rosetta Allan

A version of this work was published in *broadsheet: new new zealand poetry 15* (May 2015).

Documentary

She is full of walking. Miles flow from her toes; mud coats the first cuneiform bone. A balm she eats and eats again. Anything will do; even stones. Just to plug the maw that sits like a cavern: all-mouth, all-teeth, all-claw, all-jaw. She has nothing to feed it. Her voice is thin. Her eyes, punched holes. *This can't be happening*. It is always happening. All she can do is walk.

Ivy Alvarez

This work was previously published in *Our Own Voice* (January 2013).

Langit ang buhay

There's a hole where the nail used to be and she can see through it, straight to heaven. Oh, she's sure he's up there, somewhere, waiting for her. She peers out the hole oh the whole time we've been talking you know, peering for the epiphany only we know and have been holding onto. If only we had the guts to tell her there's no such thing: she can't make a *heaven of life*! And if it's not a gun, it's a knife, or a lie, or the phone, or a hotel room, or a stone with a key inside it. Or he might have heaven up there with him. Or she might be his wife. Better she keep looking, press her ear eye nose throat spine elbows spleen toes through the hole and ask if she fits and keep waiting for it and we can tell her stories to pass the time.

Ivy Alvarez

Author's note
Langit ang buhay: a Filipino idiom meaning 'complete happiness' (heaven of life).

This work was previously published in *Foundry* (December 2016).

Four parts blue

After reading 'The alchemy of snow', in *There's a Medical Name for This* by Kerrin P. Sharpe

Blue comes in short and ultra-short waves. Blue is a musical cliché.

We know the sea is clear, but see that she is blue. Blue collects in pools behind the iris of a candid eye. Blue may become a rose, but a rose never becomes blue.

Vincent Van Gogh painted her biography. Marco Polo found in the shimmering mountains of Badakhshan a blue more precious than gold: *blu otra mere*.

The Blessed Virgin's raiment reflects the miracle of a gauzy Fatima sun.

Yuri Gagarin described his private revelation as a pale aureole, gradually deepening blue.

This is the trick of the amorous perspective. The further away you go, the bluer my world appears.

ANITA ARLOV

Author's note
Blu otra mere was an early term for this gemstone, and was used in a mining bulletin from Marco Polo dated 1271.

A version of this work was published in *broadsheet: new new zealand poetry 15* (May 2015).

The girl who wanted to fly

She tried to tell her mum that it didn't happen the way they said, but it was hard to get her attention in a room full of people all talking at the same time and her mum's head buried in her hands and her dad standing glassy-eyed in the corner.

With her mouth right up to her mum's ear she told her she was so so so sorry about the lipstick thing because that's what made dad drag her to the sink and scrub it off with the scrubbing brush until he couldn't tell what was blood and what was lipstick and then she said she hated him and so he whacked her across the face with the back of his hand and that's why her nose turned on like a tap. But. The rest of it. Well ...

She just wanted to fly. So she made wings from chicken feathers and climbed to the top of the tree. She was a bird. She was a fairy. She flew round the sun and played tunes on the stars. She splashed rainbows on spider-silk and floated on clouds and swam with the little silver fish. She sang with frogs and waved at the moon and danced on dew-drenched grass. She was wind. She was rain. She was breath in the newborn calf.

Nobody looked pleased to see her. Nobody listened to her stories.

She watched them all pile out of the house and into the waiting black cars. She watched the neighbours lining the pavement, bowing their heads as the cars crawled past. Only one little boy noticed her standing alone on the street. As the last car turned the corner he waved to her and blew kisses from a rear window. She caught them in her cupped hands.

SANDRA ARNOLD

This work was previously published in *Fewer than 500* (September 2016).

Purse-Phone's Christmas

Persephone Chu or as her mother called her, Purse-Phone – 'You gotcha purse? You gotcha phone, Purse-Phone?' – was sick of it. Following another fight about her boyfriend, it was actually her mother who said, 'Why don't you go to Hadders!' So Purse-Phone left, slamming the door. Hadley Gould had incredibly long hair. But somehow it suggested a project and had drawn Purse-Phone in. The tattoo was what put her mother off, who had found a picture of him online. That and he looked a bit Māori. Purse-Phone's mother said so. Purse-Phone didn't reply. Hadders lived in a flat below his parents. It was Christmas Day when she appeared at the door, pissed off but embarrassed. Everybody was there. She sat on the sofa next to Hadders not saying anything. When they brought out the meal, miscellaneous relations looked at each other. Was she really going to stay for dinner? 'Grab a plate,' said Hadders. 'Once you eat, you'll be part of our family.' Which was nice. 'Forever,' his dad added. The turkey had a pomegranate glaze. Even though Hadders himself had made it, Purse-Phone found it a bit gross and a bit try-hard. She prodded it with a fork. Her phone rang. 'It's Di,' her mum said. In the corridor they came to a compromise, Hadders listening in and nodding support. She could go to Hadders's Christmas dinner next year, but now she would come home. It wasn't an apology, but it was a concession, a kindness that Purse-Phone appreciated. Hadders said something about the earth just having to circle the sun. It reminded her of her mother's nickname. She had been useless helping her daughters with their geometry homework. 'Thanks, Diameter!' Purse-Phone's sister had said. Hadders made a laugh noise at the story and Purse-Phone realised it wasn't that funny.

Nick Ascroft

Meditation

Dawdle around the estuary intending to walk up St Andrews Hill. Rest, feet dangling. Wonder if the tide is on its way. Breathe in. Observe the stones in the wall slapped by water. Water ruffled by the Norwester. Breathe out. I sit beneath the lone tree.

> yacht
> bird
> heading east

Water close to my soles. Must be coming in. That rock is still uncovered. Focus. Breathe in. Concentrate on this, body of hydrogen, oxygen, salt, minerals. Only a foot or two from meniscus to sand. It could be deep as dolphins. Breathe out. Shoals of fish, flicking colour in another direction.

> aeroplane trails banner
> dog lifts a leg

Lynn Tara Austin

This work was previously published in *Kokako 11* (2009).

Ain't chicken

Another bullet hissed over the dump. Ricky missed the seagull by a mile.

He reckoned he shot good, considering the gun was tall as him. Jem wasn't allowed anywhere near it: no knowing what she'd do. She emerged from behind a pile of rubbish, holding a can that bulged from the side. It was huge, even bigger than the ones of baked beans they cook up for school breakfast.

Jem pulled the label off and shook it in his face. 'It's a whole chook!'

'Fuck off it is,' he argued, before remembering the time she said she was going to kick him in the dick and then kicked him in the dick. Girl didn't stuff around. 'In a tin?'

'Listen.' She flicked the swollen metal and it plinked real loud. 'It's gonna blow. Watch this.'

When she chucked it at the concrete Ricky screwed his eyes shut. He opened them to dented can and a frowning sister.

'Shoot it,' she said, 'I'll hold it up.'

'Nah, that's dumb.'

'Come on! Dad said don't be a pussy,' she said, walking away across the dump.

He rested on a mouldy cushion and took aim. Jem held the can above her head, and the gunsight drifted around it until Jem raised an impatient middle finger.

He pulled the trigger.

The can exploded.

Jem grinned through the descending mist of bone and giblet. She held what was left to her chest – a jagged aluminium rose, blooming over her heart.

Sam Averis

This work was previously published in *Flash Frontier* (November 2016).

Gastrolith

One: Food

- Breakfast
  - Weetbix
  - Cup of tea
- Morning tea
  - Shrewsbury biscuits
  - Cup of tea
- Lunch
  - San Remo pasta snack (*alfredo*)
  - Cup of tea
- Afternoon tea
  - Smooth pebbles from the river up the valley, as many as I could stand. I opened my throat to let gravity tumble them into my stomach, but I couldn't stop myself swallowing. They ground against each other while my oesophagus forced them downward.
  - Handfuls of water, so cold my lips turned blue and my tongue felt too big for my mouth. It soaked my beard, and left a shiny bead on the end of each bristle. I took off my shoes and waded out into the rapids. With each step I felt them rattling around the bottom of my belly. I curled my toes to try to burrow down into the silt bed but I'm still not ready, not yet.
- Dinner *(forthcoming)*
  - Choice of pork or beef down at the RSA
  - Quiet jug of Speights in the corner

Two: Species that swallow stones

- Dinosaurs *(extinct)*
    - Caudipteryx zoui *(extinct)*
    - Cedarosaurus *(extinct)*
- Mammals
    - Whales
    - Seals
    - Humans
        - David Fitzpatrick
        - Lily Fitzpatrick. Whenever she did it I'd pick through her nappy with a fork. I never found them. The GP was a mate. He said don't worry, Dave, they'll pass eventually. But each day when I picked her up she was heavier.
    - Sea lions
- Amphibians
    - The axolotl swallows stones to control its buoyancy. It regenerates limbs, and drags itself onto land when its habitat is threatened.
    - Tadpoles

Three: Those that lie still on the bottom of the river

- Lily Fitzpatrick *(extinct)*
- Stones, polished glossy by rushing waters. Their quartz seams and bright colours sharpened by the wet.
- David Fitzpatrick *(forthcoming)*

Sam Averis

Nafanua goes to bed with her cousin

Nafanua goes to bed with her cousin, of course it's not right, but it's not new either. He is unkind and there is between them the kind of hunger that inhabits dogs when they can smell meat, have it rubbed across their muzzles, but neverever eat.
It makes them bite themselves.

Nafanua seems to think pulling up the sheet will hide them

cousin in the other bed, cousin in the hall lying with his feet up against the doorframe,
cousin's ex wife and her children sitting on the edge of the bed saying
Look I have nothing against you, cuz, but what the fuck are you doing?

TUSIATA AVIA

This work was previously published in *trout 14* (2006).

Post-ute

There is a woman with a manifesto and it says: *You will have a baby*, like it had been decreed by someone, a king of the galaxy, who can look ahead, see into time and say, *You will have a baby.* There is no woman, but there is a baby in the back of a ute. There is no baby because there is a dead baby. There are police and there is an investigation and they are investigating a dead baby in the back of a ute. There is a post-mortem and the police are waiting. There is no list of suspects but there are announcements going out from the radio asking anyone who has seen a pregnant woman who now has no baby and anyone who has no reasonable reason to have no baby to ring them immediately. There is a problem for the police, who find it hard to charge a woman with no baby, but they will try, they will try their best. There are rays going out from the radio, there are rays going out to the moon, to the solar system, to the galaxy, to the king of the galaxy, past the king of the galaxy, and way, way out to the ends of the universe.

TUSIATA AVIA

This work was previously published in *Fale Aitu/Spirit House* (VUP, 2016).

rope

He roped me, he roped me twice, the second time
it caught, fell at the right angle and landed around the bones
of my dress. He roped me from the East like light rising, from the
West like light falling, in the arrangement of his cutlery,
the bubbling land moving on its plates. Without words
or entertainment and without true silence he
roped me in the mud, in the kind of mud people call sucking,
or stinking, it sticks to one's body, one's feathers and folds.
I couldn't bear the thought of soup or vast pastures, he roped me
without heart or dancing, when he called me his *wriggly little girl.*
It was like freezing, when he roped me, I watched a thousand
doors clap shut in the clouds. He roped me and began to pull,
in spite of his own injuries, and I allowed him to be lonely.
With a shovel I buried the turquoise feathers, warm from the sun,
winter in the blood. In my mind I wrote letters to all those I'd
wronged *I want to be buried with a family resemblance.*

HINEMOANA BAKER

Author's note
This poem takes its recurring motif, and the first words of the penultimate line, from the novel *Winter in the Blood* by Blackfeet writer James Welch (Penguin, 2008).

This work was previously published in *Best New Zealand Poems 2013* (IIML, 2013).

Lullaby

The woman next door sings so slowly someone must have died. She practices her sorry aria through the walls. When we bump on the steps she is neighbourly, maybe, with her purpled eyes. She tries for lightness. The radio tells me it is snowing somewhere south. Drifts fall down for days. The presenter uses the word ghastly far too often. In the ghastly snow, he says, animals dig for their calves. When we meet on the path my own voice is chestnut and dumb. 'It's a *ghastly* thing,' I say. 'It was a ghastly mistake.' In the dark the woman's voice touches a sweet, high place. It's a small cupboard where her children once hid when she'd tried to explain – which you never really can – why the animals must paw in the cold, brown slush. Where are the young? Who hears their low, fallow voices?

SARAH JANE BARNETT

This work was previously published in *A Man Runs into a Woman* (Hue & Cry Press, 2012).

Pigeons

One morning, probably in autumn, a pigeon appeared on my back porch. I don't know where it came from, but it was pecking at the dry nuts of cat food we'd put out earlier. It – maybe a he – looked like an average pigeon, with its wings banded black, its small bobbing head tinged green. It was curiously beautiful, but I was afraid to touch the smooth, grey back as it danced around the pile of dried meat. Its feet skittered. I remembered that, during the war, homing pigeons delivered their messages even after being shot in the wing or breast. Pigeons were given names like *Paddy* and *William of Orange*, and received medals for valour in a ceremony at Buckingham Palace. People bent their necks to kiss pigeon heads. This bird could have been descended from one of those pigeons. Its delicate frame was neatly dressed in loose and shiny feathers. Its tail could almost be called a fan. It was small enough to fit in my hands. I tried to catch the bird's black alien eye, to see myself seen. To see it seeing myself seeing. In the chilled air its beak went on hammering at the dried meat.

Sarah Jane Barnett

Beach holiday

Gem knew now why her mother had always hated the beach.

There were the children, whining in the sand. There were the budgie smugglers, the voluptuous bikini girls, the miscellaneous strutters. And the skinny surfer mothers dandling their beautiful babies in the breakers, trailed by glamorous mothers-in-law in bling and white muslin.

And the dads, tiny dots out to sea, diving like dolphins, bodysurfing.

Beside Gem, on a sunlounger, her husband's friend's wife got sand between the pages of her romance.

Another towel over, her husband's friend's teenage daughter exposed more of herself than her mother could comfortably stomach, evenly sunburning each side of her body.

Gem's gritty-faced toddler kept ambling up and pulling a big white tit out of his mum's saggy togs for another feed. She felt sand around her nipple, sunscreen and ice cream and sticky mango against her skin. He wiggled across the soft marbly steps of her tummy. After thirty seconds or so he'd pull away, flashing her shapelessness to the world.

Gem's husband's friend made plenty of money and the family liked to invite their friends on holidays that allowed this to be conspicuous.

Gem's husband's friend's wife had not breastfed any of her children when they were toddlers.

Last summer was worse: the toddler, who'd been a baby then, would get distracted halfway through a feed, pull away and push down sharply on her full breast.

Last summer Gem had accidentally spray-milked the pages of her husband's friend's wife's romance.

Here were the dads, resurfacing, wandering in grinning, dawdling as they discussed the surf and perved at the surfer mothers' flat, tea-brown backsides.

Gem's husband gave her a cold, wet kiss on the forehead, like the kiss of an enormous dead fish.

'This is great,' he said. 'Let's come here again next year.'

Airini Beautrais

A version of this work was published in *The New Zealand Listener* (20 February 2017).

Tandem

A tandem bicycle is sweet but impractical. I sit on the back, my pink skirt billowing out around me. Wobbling across the tricky intersection, down Cuba Mall through gaps in the pedestrian traffic. Out onto the waterfront where the sea breeze makes my attire even more ridiculous. 'That chick's tailgating hard out,' says a passing youth to his friend. We stop and sit for a while, our conversation fractured. Fantasies never really come alive. There is always the chain catching your clothing, and the feeling that your feet are being turned by someone else's pedals. And the sea – well the sea always looks like that, is never truly sympathetic.

Airini Beautrais

This work was previously published in *Secret Heart* (VUP, 2006).

It was a teenage wedding

Some people have it. I'm thinking Travolta in *Pulp Fiction*, him and Uma Thurman when they get up and twist and everything stops. Not quite dancing, just projecting their über-coolness. Like everyone else is lesser, shadows that stare vacantly witnessing something magnificent.

Franny had it. She sashayed into the room and side-swiped her way into our booth. She wasn't even slightly self-conscious. Didn't miss a beat when she flicked me a look that made me feel I'd been punched. I fell hard. Zeb had picked up on it too, his face radiating like the booth seats, the leather squeaking as he wriggled around in his 501s. Sit still, Zeb, or you'll spook her.

Franny was talking at us in a singsong sort of way – 'affected', you might say, but this added to her appeal. Zeb knew her from college; she was a drama student, no surprises there. They were the alien beings we watched from a distance, the sort you knew you'd never get a look in with. But she was watching me. I had a bit of an epiphany, my life flashing before me like the trains on the tube when you get down the stairs too late.

She said, 'Wanna dance?'

Like I said, I'd seen *Pulp Fiction* and in some incredible twist of fate, yeah right, she hadn't. And when I took her hand and we began to dance, I forgot I was nineteen and a bit of a geek and I – I had it too.

CARRIE BECKWITH

This work was previously published in *Flash Frontier* (February 2016).

Man looking at trees

Over the road in the park there is a man looking at trees. He walks around looking up at them and when he is finished looking at one he turns away, only to find another, so he heads on over for a closer look, walks around it, head back, gazing upwards. He might be thinking about how beautiful are the trees. How wondrous nature is. He might be bringing God into it. He might be thinking words like *height* and *girth* or he might just have green on his mind. He is wondering about these trees. He might be thinking about how good it would feel to chop these trees down, about the feel of the blade against the trunk. It might be blue he has on his mind and he might be thinking about how good the sky would look if there weren't all these trees in the way.

JENNY BORNHOLDT

This work was previously published in *Sport 4* (1990) and *Waiting Shelter* (VUP, 1991).

Climate change lecture

The woman next to me doesn't like walking; nor does she read books. What she does like is travel overseas with tourist groups. She names countries she has visited. She lists places she plans to visit.

'And our country?' I ask, hopefully.

'I've seen it,' she says.

receding glacier   a tourist plane lands

NOLA BORRELL

A version of this work was published in *Kokako 24* (April 2016).

The world needs a plumber

I trudge up apartment stairs and my knees ache. The world doesn't need ACC refusing to treat me, forcing me to work in agony.

The scared Ethiopian family with the burst boiler have Jesus tacked across all their windows. The world doesn't need Jesus getting mouldy.

My rate is $95 per hour. No one needs that.

Their hot water cupboard's crammed with boxes of Weet-Bix. Can't get them wet. Musta been on special, that's what they're living on. The world doesn't need refugees eating prison food.

The world needs a plumber, who'll do the job for free. Maybe score some complimentary Weet-Bix.

MICHAEL BOTUR

This work was previously published in *Flash Frontier* (December 2015).

Mental health day

It's the second presidential debate and I'm streaming it, lying on the sofa, but I don't need pictures so I'm scrolling through Upper Clutha Trading Post, casually adding Likes. A singlet with a brown bear hugging a little red girl. Skis, 159cm, used four times. No bindings. Hillary has policy on her mind. Donald's all like *it's just words*. And there's a drum kit and it's shitty, I know, but boy is it cheap so I check some reviews, mentally scanning the space in the front room for the necessary set-up. Of course it can be done. I message for the drum kit, with two thumbs while yelling at the laptop in the corner. *Answer the question! Answer the question!* What has the world come to? The screen goes static, the birds suddenly loud outside, a lone magpie hopping on the grass.

LIZ BRESLIN

defrost the dog

defrost the dog's dinner he's on raw and must always have tripe with bones pick up from piano drop get someone to pick up from soccer drop kick pick up defrost defreeze soak some beans he's wanting to learn the cello learn to read the bass clef beans and pick up faster drop the dog's dinner pick up the cello kick the dog out he's biting the furniture cook the beans up takes six hours no hard balls in the house please kick and chase and better use a can we play mums let's play mums you be I'll be no I want to be no *I* want drop kick get the washing in wash beans hands no tripe no time for more *tripe* but maybe … pick me up?

SARAH BROOM

This work was previously published in *Gleam* (AUP, 2013).

Bro story

I'm on the road. Doing this gig, having a break at the bar. Bro comes up to me, says, 'Where you from, bro?' Bros always want to know where you from before they want to know who you are. I say, 'Nowhere in particular, bro.' Bro says, 'That's the same as everywhere in general, eh, bro?' I say, 'Yeah, spose it must be, bro.' Bro says, 'No suppose about it, bro, cos I'm from the same place. We must be whānau, eh?' I say, 'Yeah, must be, bro.' Bro looks at me and says, 'You got the mana, bro…' He's asking a question, not making a statement. I say, 'We born with the mana.' Bro says, 'Yeah, but did you keep it?' I say, 'Bro, that's a heavy question.' Bro says, 'That's the only kind of question worth asking.' So I have to pause for some consideration. I have to get introspective. Glib answers don't cut it with the heavy questions. I have to search my soul, I have to investigate the wairua, I have to pick that scab. Bro says, 'Well, bro, did you keep it?' I say, 'Bro, I'm thinking on it.' Bro says, 'Well, while you're thinking, must be your shout, eh.'

Ben Brown

A version of this work was published in *Between the Kindling and the Blaze* (Anahera Press, 2013).

Every now and then I have another child

She doesn't have a name. I'm not sure she's real. Every now and then, when I think it's time, I try to feed her warm milk, not my own. I've dried up, as is to be expected; what was I thinking of, having a baby at my age? Her eyes are shut but her mouth is open like the doll I once owned. 'Who are you?' I yell, but she's gone in deep to the other side. To follow her will kill me, there's no oxygen down there. I stand on the edge of the pit, calling out the name I have not given her and do not know. For now, I will leave her underground and close to my chest, because a character, if not a baby, can be in two places at once.

Haven't you sometimes found yourself on the edge of a lake or skyscraper with no memory of how you got there? And yet you know it's not dementia, it's more like you've slipped into another life, running on a parallel track, one layer behind. In this life I wander the streets of the city I used to live in, looking for the man who offered to take the baby to a place of safety, though he was a stranger to me. Perhaps he could see I was not up to mothering. Across the road, with their hands twitching on batons, police stand by, watching the homeless rioting. A fire engine drives onto the footpath heading straight for me. The fireman screams, 'Get out of the fucking way, lady!' I yell, 'I've got a baby!' but these days no one gives up their seat for nursing mothers. I wonder again if the baby's real. But we all feel like that when we're handed a white-wrapped bundle that the midwife says belongs to us now and forever.

Diane Brown

Starlings

I crested the hill and saw the smoke, I could see a figure struggling up the field to the road, stumbling on unseen clods of sun-hardened earth, created by his own cows in the last distant wet. The smoke was black but the flames were orange against the red paint. He was shirtless and breathless.

'Are you all right?' I asked.

We both turned as first one big tyre went 'poof', then the other. He folded his arms. His wife turned up with a miniature extinguisher, he laughed and after a pause, so did she. The diesel tank started to hiss, then the flames and the gases combined and with a whoosh the whole thing exploded. We all took a step back as a rush of hot acrid air swept up the field towards us, then a pop as first the front left and then pop again as the front right tyre went.

The tractor fell to its knees.

The grass was beginning to catch when the first fire truck arrived, then the second. There were about six cars now, though as the uniforms arrived, we drifted away, superfluous, knowing full well that we'd be moved back, away from the excitement.

I turned to look as I pulled my seatbelt on. The wife was cradling her husband from behind, rocking him gently, up on tippy-toe, propping her chin on his naked shoulder.

I googled the incident the next day. The fire service say it only takes seventeen minutes for a starling to build a nest.

Pete Carter

A version of this work was published in *Flash Frontier* (July 2015).

The anti-myth

Sometimes, when he doesn't think I'll notice, he looks me over with that sourness you see in injured runners. I think we're working well together. But his taste is all for the princely classics. When I suggest something he hasn't heard of he lets me spout about it. I was all for *'The apparition of these faces in the crowd; Petals on a wet, black bough.'* But he laughs. 'What will Mrs Shop make of that?' he says.

I have the mornings to myself. We start in the early afternoon and go late. On still evenings after dinner, the three of us go down to the terrace with our whisky. They used to go to Italy for the winter but he doesn't like the uniforms so now it's Greece. They laughed when I told them my summer plan is to go haymaking again. Then his secretary pretend whispered that 'you can't take the country out of the boy'. But I like him too. He has that prim Englishness that'd benefit from a big smacking kiss.

I met him this morning on his way back from the village. He'd been sent to dispatch a wedding telegram to the godchild. We walked up to the house together. There were thrushes in the hedge, blind dithery things. He said, 'Having you here, he loves it, someone from home.' So I asked how God's own had struck him. And then I could have kicked myself.

'He'd never take me and I wouldn't ask it,' he said.

When I got to the study we didn't start work right away. He was standing by the window holding a book, head cocked. He tossed it at me, but I caught it. Read: *The tobacco has a green smell ... autumn wind*. 'Up from the subway,' he said. 'Include them both.'

Janet Charman

Ironman

My mother kept my father in a cage.

We lived in the middle of nowhere, dark pines close-pressed against the low stone wall encircling our decaying orchard. She forbade me the forest. People died in there. At night I heard the hushing tree-breeze, corrugated crack of iron. Maybe moaning.

The day I knew, Mummy headed to town for a committee meeting.

'Lunch is gladwrapped on the table,' she said, hugging me to her studded jacket. She tore into the forest, grey hair streaming, Harley-whine fading behind her.

She'd given me a ball on my eighth birthday. Maybe I kicked too wildly. The cellar window smashed. The ball went in.

In the cellar half-light: my ball in a puddle of splinters between the fettered ankles of a rusty man: horny nails; muscled, matted chest; curtained glint of green eyes. His voice creaked.

'Hello, son.'

'Give me my ball.'

'Get the key. Under her pillow.'

Mummy's door swings open; face-powder swirls; the huge bedstead athwart crimson shag-pile; black festoons of net draped down. I slide my hand beneath her icy bolster, extract her scented hanky: '*Tabu*.' It enfolds a golden key. I freeze. For from afar I hear, homing, her Harley's mosquito-whine.

I fit the key, free the fetters, loose the chain. He grabs me, triple-strides the stairs exuding heat and yeast and hawthorn. He squints. When Mummy, shrieking, skids between the gateposts, I'm on his shoulders. We clear the wall and disappear into the darkness of the pines.

S. R. Charters

A version of this work was published in *Flash Frontier* (April 2015).

Kāinga

I share Penny's job as night porter at the Cherry Court Lodge. I never learn to work the visa machine or the floor polisher or the telephone intercom thing so I put the no vacancy sign outside and sit under the desk reading the duty manager's Freemason handbook and pray the owners don't come by. I have to make the coffee for the breakfast: three heaped tablespoons of Gregg's Instant boiled away in the percolator for at least half an hour.

I live with my boyfriend in a damp flat in Queen Street. He is part Māori and a tiny part Italian. Everyone is interested in the exotic Italian part, his fine nose. One night he was given a huge frozen block of orange roughy from this Russian sailor he'd given a lift to and we had to go round to the in-laws' place in the middle of the night to put it in their chest freezer, but no one had heard of orange roughy so no one ate it.

I share a studio behind the DIC with Rachel who has taken up Morris dancing, and Pippa who has taken up drinking at the downstairs Cook. We are on some small business scheme. We make things and try to sell them. My sister has got mixed up with Dunedin's first punk. He has green hair. There's a woman at a party with one arm. She cut the other one off to spite her boyfriend. I volunteer at the Daybreak Feminist Bookshop. There's a pack of overalled dykes and sessions on finding one's own cervix. I don't join in.

Madeleine Child

A bad relationship

Leaky homes are a big problem in New Zealand. Houses (especially those built in the midst of the 1990s) just weren't built to withstand harsh weather conditions. The outside gets to the inside, repeatedly, trapping moisture. The mould grows; the frame rots; the air around it becomes dangerous to breathe.

Homeowners all across the country have been rubbing throbbing temples, wondering how the climate has affected the skeleton of their long-term plans so horribly. See, the owners of a building are responsible for organising all remediation work, even though they merely entered the narrative part-way through. The sale of painkillers has spiked since this revelation and continues to ride a rising trend.

Common signs of a leaky home include saggy linings and a musty smell. A number of unexplained problems such as dampness and swelling are also tell-tale signs of a damaged building. There are ways to fix the mess, but the process is lengthy, costly and nothing is guaranteed. Still, most people will exhaust themselves trying.

If a homeowner decides they need help with the situation, they need to prove that the total loss of value was due to problems with the design. They need to say 'The unwarranted penetration due to inadequate resistance has really fucked things up for me,' and 'The structure is unstable, collapse after collapse, and there is no more equilibrium, anywhere.'

Once deemed eligible for assistance, the homeowner's property will be investigated. Samples will be drilled out and workers will evaluate the extent of the damage. They'll look into the people who took part in every step of the building process, before publishing the results of the mediation online, for the public to view. Evidence is very important.

Joanna Cho

She asked me if she took one pill for her heart and one pill for her hips and one pill for her chest and one pill for her blood how come they would all know which part of her body they should go to

I explained to her that active metabolites in each pharmaceutical would adapt a spatial configuration leading to an exact interface with the receptor molecules on the cellular surfaces of the target structures involved.

She told me not to bullshit her.

I told her that each pill had a different shape and that each part of her body had a different shape and that the pills would only work when both these shapes could fit together.

She said I had no right to talk about the shape of her body.

I said that each pill was a key and that her body was ten thousand locks.

She said she wasn't going to swallow that.

I told her that they worked by magic.

She asked me why I didn't say that in the first place.

Glenn Colquhoun

This work was previously published in *Playing God* (Steele Roberts, 2003).

White night

A woman in a red velvet coat hoots with laughter. There are men in floral shirts and dress pants. The Sky Tower is pewter against the grey sky. It feels like Gotham City.

Everyone has somewhere to go, something to see.

On Lorne Street, it's a different crowd. The concrete feels gritty. Robert reads poems about love on the library steps, while a homeless man with his bedding piled on a carrier cycles by. In the crowd is a couple in high-vis vests: the man with a polo shirt and a beer paunch. Kids lounge in bean bags, and seem to be listening. An old man, with a Zimmer frame, and a guitar on his back, stays nearly all night. A forest is projected onto the wall above us.

Poems about growing up in damp houses, about parents in prison, about drugs.

A group of cyclists, all lit up, gather at the end of the street. They've been on the Light Path. Yay for Len Brown and liveability. I cross at the lights with an astronaut, and a bevy of beautiful bodies in silver spangles.

Back at the festival garden, my children emerge from a circus tent. There is an overwhelming waft of paint fumes. I wait in line for a glass of Stoneleigh Pinot Gris. The man ahead of me says to the bartender, 'I'm doing a movie right now. That's why you didn't recognise me. My hair was black the last time we met.' I sneak a look in case it is someone I should recognise. It isn't.

Carolyn Cossey

Still life

The sky is a wall of steel. No feeling, only grey. No breeze, no rain, just diminished light. Cresting the hill the black, winter-stripped trees stab the sky with sharp, twisted branches.

There's too much silence in the car; a need to fill the air with words.

'We shouldn't have told your mother,' Sarah says. She takes a sharp breath in.

'Hush now,' Mark says. 'It will be okay.'

His voice is a calm lake to float upon. He's driving very smoothly, gliding along, slowing down to take the corner.

Sarah watches the world go by the window, the fields, the cars, the pavements; a woman in a red coat entering a shop. And all of it bathed in this fading day. Behind the grey mountain of clouds, on another horizon, there's probably a glorious Turner sunset.

At the hospital the two of them are asked to wait in line for a second, seemingly pointless, scan.

'They find truth in their machines,' she says. But Mark is silent now. He's retreated behind a magazine. Eventually a nurse calls her name.

On the screen a small, still shape.

It's a stark composition, in black and white, yet so perfectly framed. And all Sarah can do is wonder, who could have pictured this treacherous, beautiful world? And who, seeing some small mistake, could have erased this half-drawn miracle?

Outside the dark is gathering and the clouds have dispersed. Later, frost will make patterns on the roofs of cars, intricate and repeating as if by design.

Celia Coyne

The man who kissed his wife

The boy who was too drunk to drive (because his girlfriend had left him with a broken heart and a bottle of vodka) drove as if walking a tightrope, scared of falling.

The woman who was running late (because her husband had caught her in the bedroom and kissed the side of her neck) strapped her child into the back of the car and drove hurriedly towards the day-care centre.

The dairy owner who was going bankrupt (thanks to regular visits from seasoned shoplifters) stood on the pavement smoking a cigarette and watching the passing traffic.

The dairy owner saw the boy who was too drunk to drive coming down the road. He recognised the car – one of the criminals, one of the bastards. He got his phone out to take a picture, catch the number plate.

The child of the woman who was running late started to cry as she realised she had left her bunny on the hallway floor. The woman turned to soothe her. The boy who was too drunk swerved to avoid the dairy owner he stole food from, who had stepped off the kerb with the camera phone. The boy felt himself falling from the tightrope into a wide space.

The woman who was running late turned back from soothing her child who had lost her bunny to see the boy who was too drunk cross the centre line. The dairy owner watched with his phone in his hand. The boy, the woman, the child, metal on metal, rubber on tarmac, flesh, bone, metal, rubber, tarmac. Silence. Screaming.

The man who had kissed his wife's neck and then held her lovingly for two minutes too long sat down at his desk and reached out to touch a photo of his wife and child, smiling.

Caroline Crick

This work was previously published in *Flash Frontier* (July 2013).

Shells

One minute the shells were in her hand. Then, in a sudden stumble, were scattered on the beach. Amongst hundreds of similar shells.

The collecting had been taking place all day. The older brothers and sisters had chided her for it, told her that as soon as she got home Mum would throw the shells out, just as she always did. Before the child had even forgotten about them.

This collection was particular. Each shell had some individual feature that connected with the rest. This was a connected collection, she insisted. Her oldest brother sneered at her use of big words. Did she even know what she was talking about? He laughed at her and then, with his six sleek teenage mates, raced to the waves, crashed into them in an upturned waterfall.

She stared at the shells, trying to see which ones had been hers.

A dog, one of those long-haired bouncing dogs oblivious to what they're trampling underfoot, came rushing in amongst the family, shouted at by its owners further along the beach, shouted and shooed away by the rest of the family, raced after by Danny with joyful hilarity.

The shells were now obscured by sand, mixed thoroughly with shells that hadn't found favour.

She refused to cry. And who would have noticed if she had? Tears were disregarded even when cuts and falls and breaks occurred.

She gazed at the sand, the shells.

And picked up the first.

The second.

The third.

Mike Crowl

This work was previously published in *Flash Frontier* (April 2014).

A life lived

My life has stopped because my sister is dead. I miss her, of course, although that's a pathetic understatement. It's as if I've lost a limb; some day I may learn to live without it, but its absence will always be felt.

Ever since that day a year ago when Meghan left the house with lies on her lips, I notice Mum doesn't quite look me in the eye. I realise it's because every day I look more like *her*, and instead of being a blessing, it is the cause of my mum's undoing.

'Mum. I'm going out.' It's a statement. If I form it as a question, ask for permission, I've already lost.

'Where?' Mum asks. Her eyes pool with tears, and I sigh inwardly.

'To Kathy's. We talked about it a couple of weeks ago.' This is a lie. But Mum will just assume she's zoned out again.

'Who else is going?'

'Just the usual.'

'Will there be drinking?' This is *the* question.

'Yes, Mum, but I won't drink,' I say. Another lie.

I wait for an answer. It doesn't come.

Mum inches away from me, as if I'm a snake ready to strike. Avoiding eye contact she shuffles the mail on the bench and takes a step back. She closes the open pantry and takes another step towards the hallway. Turning slightly she adds something to the shopping list on the fridge by the door.

And then she disappears completely.

Nikki Crutchley

A version of this work was published in *Flash Frontier* (June 2016).

Bus stop

Mum said the universe had given her a sign. I didn't think the universe was equipped for sign giving so I'm not sure what that meant. What I think she might have meant was that God had given her a sign. But Mum didn't believe in God. She and I agreed on that. So what I think she really meant was that she was looking for a sign.

Anyway, while waiting at the bus stop Mum saw a construction worker with the words 'One Life' tattooed on his forearm and she decided to leave Dad. Proving if nothing else that Georgia, who was a believer, was onto something with the whole seek and ye shall find thing. But in the end it was Dad who left Mum.

He left her after she vacuumed during a dinner party.

Daniel said that that wasn't why he left her. That it was merely emblematic of all the things that drove him out. That vacuuming was just the straw that broke the camel's back. I got that, even though I sometimes suspected that Daniel suspected I didn't. My point was that if a straw was required, and without that one straw the camel's back would still be intact, then it followed that it was the vacuuming that caused Dad to leave. Daniel said if it hadn't been the vacuuming, it would have been something else, but I thought, tell that to the camel.

Lilla Csorgo

A version of this work was published in *North & South* (April 2014).

Two sparrows

I hold my feet above water. I balance my calves against the walls of the bath. I want to lie back in the water, let the water lap around my ears, but I'll lose my balance. I hold tight with my right hand to the side of the bath, and use my left to lather the soap against my shoulder, my breast, my stomach.

The bandages on my feet sag. I wash my legs, but then my calves won't stick to the side of the bath, they keep slipping. I flex my stomach to keep my feet out of the bath.

'I'm done now!' I call. My voice sounds tinny in the tiled bathroom. I watch two sparrows on the windowsill. I like the way they hop on their little kneeless legs.

She helps me out of the bath and into a wheelchair draped with a huge towel. I don't look at her. She says I got the bandages wet. No, I tell her, I didn't let my feet in the water at all. I was very, very careful.

'I don't want to look,' I say.

'Maybe they'll look better today.'

'They won't.'

Her hands are gentle, soft. We don't touch much now. It's me I think. At first she was the same as before but I didn't want it. I miss her now. I take her hand and kiss her fingers. She smiles at me.

She leans up and kisses me full on the lips.

'You're getting better,' she says.

'But not my feet.'

She unwraps my bandages as the nurses taught her. I don't watch. I feel a surge of hope as she peels off the last length. But nothing is different, her breath stays even, she says nothing.

'Maybe not your feet, but you're getting better.'

Makyla Curtis

Vive le roi

I am the lion. I have a place to sit and even the concrete path stays away from that place. I can sit there. The place is a little tree and my sneakers slip on its trunk as I watch the grown-ups rushing. They must be rushing to buy brown trousers. They have filled the hall with people and they are serving food. I cannot go there because there are no seats next to her so what is the point?

I am the lion. One of the old ones beckons me from my place. I am hungry so I think I might eat her. The food sounds nice. I join the queue but most of the food is gone already. The plates are very clean. As I wait in line I look around and there she is. The seats by her are taken. She sees me looking and smiles. When she sleeps I know because I can feel her dreams. They crowd up against me, gently pushing on my lips.

I am the lion. I am all full so I rest and she speaks to people who aren't me. I watch carefully so she will not see. They are talking about an argument from last night. I wish I was there, I would have helped, I would have saved her.

I am the lion. The old ones collect around me. I am special but I know that just means different. When they cuddle me I do not flinch because they cannot change me. Tomorrow I will still be the lion.

Morgan Davie

This work was previously published in Morgan Davie, Jane Elizabeth, Dan Rabarts and Stephen Rhoades, *Urban Driftwood* (Dan Rabarts, 2009).

Schrödinger's cat

Schrödinger's cat stretches in front of the fire, contemplating the meaning of life and death.

Erwin has gone out to a lecture. He'll come back later. He always does. He has to. Schrödinger's cat licks one paw, rubbing it behind her left ear. Erwin went with Anny. He said he wouldn't be late.

Schrödinger's cat methodically cleans her fur. In the hall, the clock strikes midnight. A thought trickles its way through the cat's mind. Perhaps Erwin isn't coming home. Maybe he's lying in a ditch somewhere having one of his coughing fits. Perhaps he's been poisoned, or had a heart attack, or been struck by a meteorite. What are the chances of that? Maybe Erwin is already dead. What will she do then? Who will look after Schrödinger's cat, if Erwin doesn't come home? Anny never liked cats.

Schrödinger's cat doesn't dare look outside, to search for Erwin. What if she distracts him? What if he sees her and steps out into the road in front of a speeding bicycle, or trips over a pothole and cracks his head? Then it would be her fault. That he is dead. No. Safest to sit still. Best not to look. After all, it might affect the outcome. He will come back. He always does.

Schrödinger's cat curls up in her new box, with that strange orange and black symbol painted on the outside. She falls asleep. While the clock ticks, Schrödinger's cat dreams about life and death.

Simultaneously.

Melanie Dixon

A version of this work was published in *Flash Frontier* (September 2015).

What the science tells us

The science tells us that 8 out of 10 cats prefer Whiskas, that there is a 50:50 chance of having a boy or a girl, that ovulating women wear red. Science tells us that a big earthquake is overdue in Wellington, that suicide is one of the most common causes of death for teenagers, that you're safer if you wear a seatbelt.

Science tells us that love is real, people fall in and out as easily as getting on or off a bus. If you're single, it's only bad luck. Does that make you feel any better? Science tells us that boy meets girl, Romeo will fall in love with Juliet, and an infinite number of monkeys will tell us the same thing.

Plants grow towards the sun, darkness is the absence of light, black is not white. Science puts two highly reactive gases together to make a molecule we can't live without. It tells us a cat in a box can be simultaneously dead and alive.

Science gives us quarks, mesons, gravitons, anti-matter, black dwarves. It tells us we're all made of particles from the last supernova. Every human being. Star dust.

But science can't make my morning coffee, or scratch my back in the shower. It can't ask me about my day. It can't tell me why you left.

Science tells us we are made of string in a multidimensional spacetime continuum. It gives us infinite worlds with infinite outcomes.

In a parallel universe, we are still together.

Melanie Dixon

The smell of it all

John sat to finish *Paradise Lost* with those ulcerated lips, those blind eyes, those pinched, gritted kidneys. Ribs rutted his chest. Food: repulsive. That pelican daughter, the quill in her fingertips stained with ink and blood – the smell of it all, flesh like wet clay. He spoke his poem, already written, already read. It was inked into eternity through that girl's bone and skin, her tendons, throbs of wet brainwork, nauseating pulp. He read the world into symmetry, his body to poverty, his daughter to death, his poem and name into rock and sky.

ALLAN DREW

This work was previously published in *Flash Frontier* (December 2015).

Islands and cities

The neighbourhood I live in is next to the Spicer landfill in Porirua. Twice a day, every day, flocks of crisp seagulls fly all the way down the street from the tip – over my school, past the mall my sister works at, across the skate park and the flyover.

They carry bones, McDonald's wrappers, tampons and plastic in their cherry beaks and red feet. Sometimes they drop bits on my house.

The bones make a special flat clang against the corrugated iron, like the marrow inside stops them from echoing. Dad runs outside with the hose when he can get out of his chair in time, but the seagulls don't care about water.

'Useless flying rats,' he says. 'It's a disgrace.'

I think most animals that share spaces with people have a purpose. Cats and dogs are supposed to love us so we take care of them, but sparrows, pigeons, blackbirds and seagulls fit around us without being asked. It's why I like them – they're beautiful for no reason.

One day I went out to watch them bring in the dawn, and they never came. I waited until the sun came out and the rubbish from yesterday started to stink.

Over breakfast, Dad said the men at Spicer's had poisoned them with a narcotic paste and he was sorry. I said it wasn't fair and my sister said they deserved to be shot, but when Dad saw my face, he told me to get in the car.

At the landfill, hundreds of cool white bodies lay limp across the rubbish. They were so clean, they blocked out everybody's mess with the weight of their feathers.

Dad put his hand on my shoulder. I put my hands over my eyes and the black light white of the birds was still there.

Sarah Dunn

This work was previously published in *Flash Frontier* (July 2014).

Optimism

When I got to the cinema I waited for the film to begin. When the film began I waited for it to affect me. When I found I was not being affected, I waited for the film to end. When the lights came up I waited for other people to leave before I put on my coat and gathered my belongings. Then I drove home waiting to reflect on the substance of the film and the impact it might have on my life. While I was waiting for that to happen, I drove to the supermarket and waited in a queue to buy bread. This was to avoid waiting in a queue tomorrow to buy a sandwich. When I got home I found I was too tired to analyse the film, and thought it could wait until the morning. Then I could write something about it while waiting for the bus. I put the jug on and waited for it to boil while brushing my teeth. I made tea and went to bed. I must have fallen asleep waiting for the tea to cool because this morning when I woke up, I saw it had spilt over the book that I was going to write about the film in. I would have to wait for it to dry.

Lynley Edmeades

This work was previously published in *As the Verb Tenses* (OUP, 2016).

Leftovers

Janet isn't sure if it is her stomach or bladder that has woken her. One must be dealt with before the other. She takes the deep breath that will move her body from the bed and puts her feet on the floor.

Rod lies awake, eyes closed, breathing evenly. He hears his wife's footsteps as she leaves the bedroom, shuts the toilet door, urinates, water on water. This goes on for minutes, it is torture: *water torture*, he thinks.

Janet has flushed the toilet. She heads to the kitchen, pushes at the door. Is it locked? She turns the handle. Nothing. She can hear the fridge groaning. Calling to her. Earlier in daylight, while grass was mowed, birds called, and in the heaviness of afternoon sleep, she stumbled through dreams of red meat.

Rod has gone back to sleep. He doesn't hear Janet leave the house, her footsteps as feet crunch gravel, the keys in the lock, the back door opening.

The sun is up. Janet sleeps. Rod notices a faint smell of gravy. He is out of bed, and unlocking the kitchen door. Roast beef sandwiches he thinks. He rubs his eyes and sees half eaten roast potatoes, dried crusts of bread, an apple and his roast beef, lumps strewn across the kitchen floor. There are sandy footprints; the back door is open. He steps back, acid in his throat; his heart leaps in his chest. Then he remembers the smell of his sleeping wife.

Rod cleans. Janet sleeps.

Annette Edwards-Hill

A version of this work was published in *Flash Frontier* (April 2014).

Coming attractions

The trouble is, all the stories seem to come from the past. It would be easy to go on unearthing fragments from its rich midden, fitting words to them, making them seem to speak for themselves. Bringing them to life again.

But if grandmothers and mothers are anything to go by, she's got at least another twenty years. She doesn't want to spend them walking backwards; she wants to stumble across new stories, sticking out of the ground ahead of her, tripping her up and making her catch her breath. She just has to work out how to reach them.

Anne Else

This work was previously published in *Flash Frontier* (December 2016).

Antarctica

The man finds the boy in a drainpipe and when he asks him *what are you doing in there?* the boy looks at him as if he should already know and says *I'm looking for Antarctica.* Later at home, the man's wife catches him staring at the tiny specks of dust spiralling in the late-afternoon sun and when she asks *what are you thinking?* for about the millionth time he hates her but he also knows he'd hate it even more if she stopped asking so he shrugs and says *I'm thinking about Antarctica.*

He goes back the next day and the boy is gone. He waits for him because he knows there's something they needed to say but forgot. The sky is heavy metallic: the hour before snowfall. He pulls his collar tight and heads home and when he gets there his wife's standing naked in the kitchen. It has started to snow and the only colour in the room is the orange of her fingernails. The snow falls and they can't get warm, no matter how hard they make love. Later he's staring again and his wife says *Antarctica?* but how could she know he's more than a million miles away with the boy in the drainpipe.

He returns to the drainpipe and crouches on his hands and knees. His shoulders barely fit but he wedges himself in. He is about to turn and crawl down the pipe, all the way to a new continent, when a stranger walks by and sees him and when he asks *what are you doing in there?* the man looks at the stranger as if he should already know.

MICHELLE ELVY

This work was previously published in *SmokeLong Quarterly* (April 2015).

Beer goggles

It's a long walk up between streets, a Wellington short cut, past cabbage trees and damp, tightly-planted agapanthus. The steps are dark and steep, tricky to negotiate, and Warren and Lola stumble against each other. They mug creeping up the steps, shushing and high-stepping like cartoon villains. The wind has dropped, the night turned still. Stopping to catch their beery breath, turning, they see the city below them. Closer, lights glow in scattered windows of the university buildings, patterning the sky.

As they pass a sternly locked gate, a motion sensor clicks and a light comes on. They both jump, and stop. The light surrounds them, darkness cameoing them. In the halo of light, Warren looks pasty, but nicer, better-looking than he did in the pub. Beer goggles, Lola thinks. She reaches out to him, adjusts his collar. She spits on her hand and tries to flatten his hair. She wipes his chin, makes a joke of it.

'You'll do,' she says.

'Your flatties got high ex-pect-orations, eh?'

'Shusssssh. You'll wake all the Kelburn matrons.'

A dog barks, close to them, maybe a house or two away. The sound carries on the night air, and another dog answers it, then another, off into the distance.

'Woo-woo-rooo-roo.' Warren lifts his face to the sky, eyes closed.

'Is that what Dunedin dogs say?'

'Yep. What do Wellington dogs say?'

'They say don't walk up my steps or I'll bite you. And they eat Dunedin dogs for dinner.'

The light goes off, and the dogs stop barking. Lola and Warren stand still and quiet. The darkness pulls in solid around them. Lola closes her eyes, feels the Guinness roil in her stomach, black and sharp.

Tracy Farr

A version of this work was previously published in *Flash Frontier* (July 2013).

Seven wishes

A straight account is difficult
so let me define seven wishes:

that you should fit inside me neat as the stuffing in an olive
that you should stand inside the safe circle of my eye
that you should sing, clear, on the high rock of my skull
that you should swing wide on the rope of my hair
that you should cross rivers of blood, mountains of bone
that I should touch your skin through the hole in your T-shirt
that we should exchange ordinary tales

Fiona Farrell

This work was previously published in *Cutting Out* (AUP, 1987).

Rogue trading

The first time it happened there was a magpie trying to get in at the window. They steal other birds' babies – macabre rogues. I've seen them: raiding the nests, gouging the little ones out of the guttering while the mothers shriek to the clouds and perform a death spiral like suicidal paragliders. This one took mine. When it happened again, and again, I said it was the magpies that had taken them. It made more sense than admitting I had indirectly murdered them through a starving adolescence. Everyone said I was just unlucky but mad to think so superstitiously. And then, when you were born, I knew it was true: three for a girl. They let me keep you.

RACHEL J. FENTON

This work was previously published in *Blue Five Notebook* (April 2012).

Firefighters talking to the siren they are running toward

When the siren sounds, you can see the men emerge from the doorways of the top shop and the tavern and the sandspit packet tours office, and run. They run down the street, towards the sound. *Don't stop, I'm coming*, says their speeded breath, their legs pumping a virile rhythm. For the young men, the firefighting task is akin to sex. *Wee-oh, Wee-oh.* An urgent shining redness is wailing for them. For the older men, who leave doorways running but peter out halfway down the street to a pained jog, shoulders high, gut out, they are grateful just to make it to the fire engine, which they pat like an enormous, aging red cat, before swinging themselves up inside. Because, who knows, this might be the last ride.

Joan Fleming

This work was previously published in *The Same as Yes* (VUP, 2011).

Husband and wife talk without talking at a difficult dinner party

Their elbows on the table are *yang*, their backs against the hip, uncomfortable chairs are *yang*, the jokes are witty and cruel, the bread-crust hard, the red wine sharp and showy. When she unhooks an earring and pulls at the lobe of her ear, he knows she has a headache. When he starts shredding the paper napkin, she knows he is thinking about his father's jumpy, medicated heart. He drinks more, and she stops drinking. It is for the same reason. Her earring tings against an empty wine glass. His father, miles away, tosses in his sleep. Underneath the table, their bare feet find each other, *yin*, arch against arch, making a soft space where speech can grow, in the darkness.

JOAN FLEMING

This work was previously published in *The Same as Yes* (VUP, 2011).

Alex and David

For Alex, Tuesday night became a long, winding tunnel. The podcast, *Attenborough in Paradise*, had her thinking. *Quest for something or other. All we have to do is ... down goes the counterweight. Now I'm leaving that dark world of the forest.* Alex was still in the dark forest. She was on a train that was travelling through one in slow motion. She had time to capture still frames in her mind. *What first drew me to the bear? One bear in particular really caught my interest. I met her when she was just a cub, thirteen years ago. It's great to see her after all this time, but does she remember me? I certainly remember her.* And so on. Alex was tossing and turning, in between yawns. She stretched her body out as long as she could under the feather duvet. David's voice. *A raffishly handsome insect with long elegant legs and a glossy black and scarlet body.* The sound of rain. Sleep evaded her.

By morning, Alex was exhausted. Exhausted. *David is from another planet. Does he even sleep? Does he hug orangutans in his dreams, in Borneo ... no wait ... Sumatra?* The room is a stage set. Just a nondescript chair and table as props. A poster of an orangutan on the wall. *Save the orangutans.* Enter stage left. Alex is enjoying her Marmite jaffle when she hears David's key in the door. Badly written script. David (addresses the audience): *In all my years of exploration these are the creatures I find most curious.*

Anna Forsyth

A version of this work was published as 'Alex is in love with David' in *n-SCRIBE 10* (September 2015).

Doors

the drinks go down, the doors open, the two say things they may not have said sober, being more open now, together, with the drinks going down, and mentioning the last time they opened like this and acknowledging to each other the existence of those doors (neither one knowing to start with, how open the doors might go)

the drinks going down some more, first that one's round and then the other's, evening it up, making it okay, talking through the open doors, saying things that couldn't be said when the doors were shut

and one to say I want you and this is how and to say they have been too much (liking) and too much (thinking about) and the other to say they like to hear that and they like the drinks going down in the company of the one, and the one to hear that

and then the doors push open a little further, wider than they've been before and wider than the one thought they'd go (but it's okay because neither will say) and it's not without apprehension (this is how), a squeeze, but once they're through, that's it

after, the drinks settle and what was said has been said and what was done has been done and the other says next time sober and so will there be? maybe there will, again, through the doors, too early to say for sure, everything altered and no returning and next time, the drinks not going down

Janis Freegard

Elephant

It was clear the elephant was going nowhere. For the third time that month, Granddad got out his tool box and started repairing the couch, this time reinforcing it with an old steel bed frame from the bowels of the basement. The elephant watched from a flattened bean bag in the corner.

Over the hammering, Grandma shouted, 'Are you sure you wouldn't like a biscuit?' and proffered a plate of afghans. But the elephant just looked at her dolefully before sucking the entire contents of Grandma's largest Crown Lynn teapot into its trunk, then spraying the lot over its big, pachyderm head.

'There haven't been any circuses in the area at all?' Grandma asked Bill when he showed up for his morning cuppa.

Bill helped himself to an afghan and settled into the one remaining armchair, opposite the elephant. It was clear he hadn't shaved. Again. He slurped his Irish breakfast tea from Grandma's favourite Temuka teacup. The elephant watched him.

'We had a postcard from Josie yesterday,' said Grandma, pointing to the mantelpiece. 'She's got a great job, Bill. And a fabulous new flat near the harbour. She's in her element.'

Bill knocked back the rest of his tea before turning his cup upside down in the saucer as he always did. 'Reckon that one's a water elephant.' He headed for the back door.

'Is that so?' said Granddad to Bill's retreating form. 'Is that so?'

Grandma looked at Granddad. 'I'll give you a hand,' she said. The old Para pool in the garage was a heavy bugger. They hadn't had it out since Josie left.

Janis Freegard

This work was previously published in *Flash Frontier* (July 2013).

My son is turning black

My son is turning black. There are strands of granite-blue running through his baby blond hair, and ruddy stains under his eyes that weren't there before.

'Wear a hat,' I say, when he leaves for school. I hope it will protect him from the sun. Everything's happening so fast.

In the evening I examine his skin for shady patches. I've started taking pictures so I can compare the new against the old. Every day, he's a tone darker. He says it's just the lighting. But lighting doesn't explain why I find great clumps of golden hair on his pillow when I make the bed.

I stand behind him when he eats his cereal, and run my fingers over his scalp, over this *otherness* that sprouts from his skin. The tight black curls are taking over. I want to shave it with a razor, but there's little I can do about the skin on his arms turning chestnut brown.

Even his lips are changing, filling out, and his nose lies flatter against the bones of his cheeks.

No one else notices. My husband doesn't understand the ramifications, my mother is unaware anything has changed.

I'm not sure he should stay with us any more.

He's different.

He's not one of us.

NOD GHOSH

Shape shifters on the bus

When Ronald McGourvey and his family of shape shifters caught the 47 to Scarborough, nobody noticed.

Timothy McGourvey had perfected becoming nitrogen-fixing bacteria, so he went as a *rhizobium*. He'd had trouble with symbiosis, but discovered he could run solo for short periods.

The bacterium was proving to be one of Timothy's favourites.

Timothy's sister Rebecca wanted to try something new. She'd been practising *Muscovy duck* for weeks, summoning forty pairs of chromosomes and an opposite spiralling cloaca. *Aspergillus* was a word Rebecca liked to roll in her mouth like a chip coated in sherbet, so she went as an *Aspergillan* fungal spore. Rebecca and her brother floated above an Asian schoolgirl's ponytail.

Vivienne McGourvey had lately found reverting back from inorganic forms problematic, so she floated onto the 47 behind her children as a curl of cellophane. She needed the experience. Vivienne sailed in eddy currents behind a lady wheeling a tartan shopping trolley bag.

Ronald watched his wife with cautious devotion. He was thinly disguised as dog dirt around a wheel of the tartan trolley.

The bus rolled on.

The bus stopped.

Passengers alighted at Scarborough, and Ronald found himself stranded. The tartan bag, with accompanying lady, stayed put. Ronald transformed into a gas and slipped through the opening doors, turning adiabatic somersaults.

Vivienne remained attached by static cling to the nylon coat of a rugby enthusiast. She flexed her transitioning apparatus, but nothing happened. Vivienne watched her children waddle and roll down the metal steps of the number 47, accompanied by delighted squeals from the Asian schoolgirl.

Timothy had transformed into a French fingerling, one of sixteen varieties of potato he'd learnt to emulate. Rebecca followed, her penguin flippers slapping her sides like wet cloths.

The Asian schoolgirl laughed.

Nobody else noticed.

Nod Ghosh

This work was previously published in *Flash Frontier* (August 2016).

Mannykin

She yanks at buttons, pulls my shirt off, hustles me into another. She throws me horizontal, pulls on shorts. *Shorts!* I hate shorts.

I loathe her – the schoolgirl.

But I love Marina – I worship her. Marina caresses as she dresses and undresses me. She smooths her olive hands down my front with the familiarity of a lover. When she zips up my fly, I want to reach down, stroke her silver hair. I would, if I could.

Marina's for the chop – I know, because I've heard the schoolgirl gossiping with the owner.

'She's past it now, she's bad for business.'

Treacherous little bitch.

Marina *moves* the merchandise. People are drawn through the door. They hum as they open their wallets. They know that music … '*Cuando Juanica y Chan Chan En el mar cernian arena; Como sacudia el 'jibe' A Chan Chan le daba pena.*'

Once, the schoolgirl asked Marina for a translation.

'When Juanica and Chan Chan sifted sand in the sea, the way she was shaking the "sieve" was driving Chan Chan mad.' The schoolgirl looked blank then scuffed to the sound-system. People stopped opening their wallets. Miley Cyrus – enough said.

Sometimes, when the schoolgirl's left, Marina dances: salsa in stocking-feet. I fantasise about breaking through this fibreglass shell, taking her in my arms. She'd be Juanica, I'd be Chan Chan. We'd both be so happy …

Tomorrow the theme is Africa. I dread the safari suit.

Céline Gibson

A version of this work was published in *Flash Frontier* (February 2016).

Geometry

He was a professor of mathematics; it was not surprising how his mind worked. He lived in a world of straight lines. His house was a rectangle filled with several cubes. He liked right angles, No acute angles – too difficult to furnish.

Everything he saw he translated into a mathematical shape or equation. To him, a corn cob was a cylinder, an apple a sphere. Bananas and pears presented a nice little mathematical puzzle to mull over at the traffic lights.

The triangle insinuated itself into his life as he tried to get through a doorway at the same time as his top maths student, Angela Bean.

In one moment she overturned all his mathematical meanderings.

She was a vision of spheres and curves, in stark contrast to the collection of cylinders and parallels that made up his wife. Over the spring he forgot about rectangles as he and Angela lay happily under spherical trees or walked hand in hand over curvaceous hills. He coached her and found her a willing student in many ways, not all of them mathematical.

She dropped him for a Zoology student right after her exam results rewarded her with straight As in maths.
He was distraught.
The triangle had been broken.
Now all he saw were acute angles.

Acute sadness. Acute loneliness. Acute feelings of betrayal.
He transferred his energies to his linear rows of peas and beans.
This lasted right through the summer holidays, until March.

The term began.
He looked over the new intake of students and there she was, in the front

row. Petite, blonde, another exquisite collection of spheres and curves. And the third side of the triangle slid back into place.

Robyn Gosset

A version of this work was published in Graeme Lay, ed., *The Third Century: new New Zealand short short stories* (Tandem Press, 1999).

Territories

The boy's mother is in the kitchen. A lace curtain billows in the open window, the breeze heavy and warm.

Below in the garden, the boy pushes the shed door. Dust glitters in the sunbeams and he can see tools hanging in rows on the wall. He touches the cold edge of an axe and shivers. Under the bench is a crate of beer which smells like his father. He crouches down and runs a finger around the wavy edge of a bottle cap. Suddenly the door swings shut with a bang. He leaps to pull it open and runs out into the sun. He looks up at the house and sees his mother through the lace curtain. She sees him too and smiles. So he kicks the shed door and laughs, to show he's not afraid. Of the dark, of the axe, of anyone.

Anna Granger

This work was the winner of the 2014 BNZ Short Short Story Award.

The argument

I went to university for a long time and learnt how to construct an argument with a beginning an end and substantial evidence but in order to survive I also hid my argument in poetry and printed it on tracing paper I dreamt my dentist had become a real estate agent and asked me to help out one Saturday but I was late as I couldn't find a parking space I liked I kept shifting away from the way a branch hung or the light fell or a window opened out I kept passing the door to the agency and seeing someone come out a woman came out and started laying large objects along the wall obstacles it seemed like a large bird kite that would only fly in a miracle I left the car at last and a woman brought the OPEN sandwich board out on to the street I wasn't sure how to explain my unreliability to the dentist real estate agent so I gave her my thesis to read and started answering the telephone in a strange voice

Paula Green

From the work 'Appointment with Sophie Calle' in *Making Lists for Frances Hodgkins* (AUP, 2007).

The moss on the sycamores …

The moss on the sycamores and on the oaks is as thick as my finger. The wedding ring has been found after two years or more lying in dust under the bed. The thin plain circlet, just in time for the anniversary. So things come back, and I turn to see my brother walking into the supermarket in Blarney. The long thin height of him, his beautiful jaw. And my eyes fill with tears as is the way with those who walk in two worlds or more at the one time, the walls between the past and the present are so thin. They walk as shadows, the dead, still themselves but silent. Walking inside the membrane of the years that are as soft as the white smoke that rises from grey trees of a certain kind that glow like hooded lanterns in the distance. An exhalation that vanishes as you approach it.

BERNADETTE HALL

This work was previously published in *Maukatere, floating mountain* (Seraph Press, 2016).

Hecate's skirt

At night by the river's edge smoke rises from the encampment. There's talk of the moon, of stars and sky people, of everything beginning and ending in cosmic dust. Maps are drawn with sticks, galaxies scratched in dry earth. In your hands you hold the shadow of the river's mouth and you wait like a salmon for the final leap that will bring you home.

Around the fire, old men sing of their own importance, of war and hunting, of following the tracks of the soft-skinned doe; old women, freed from bleeding and bearing, cradle stories, weaving memories into ballads and poems.

You swim to the surface of the river, your body as cool and poised as an arum lily; in your hands you carry your last bloodstained skirt. You return it to the river's mouth – how it once shimmered and swirled – and watch while it's carried out to sea. There it becomes Hecate's, that old goddess, her moon face waning, washed clean in the currents of time.

Trisha Hanifin

With our eyes closed we begin to dance

On Monday night I dream about Charlie Brown. He stands at the window watching Snoopy sleep on top of his kennel. Snoopy's little tummy moves up and down as he snores and he's wearing his goggles and scarf, the way he does when he's playing the Red Baron. In the background Schroeder plays a blues tune on the piano and I have this weight on my chest that makes it hard to breathe.

On Tuesday Gerry gives me an ultimatum. The glasses or him, he says. Twenty-five pairs is twenty-four too many.

'What's brought this on,' I say?

'A bloody new pair every month for the last two years.'

'I pay for them out of my own money.'

'That's not the point.'

'What *is* the point?'

'It's crazy,' he says. 'Sick in the head.'

My new glasses slide down my nose. Gerry's a blur on the other side of the kitchen table. I grope towards the bathroom and sit on the toilet seat. The back door slams. I blow my nose, go into the bedroom to find another pair of glasses – tinted, to soften the glare.

A text arrives from Gerry saying he's at his mother's.

I spread my glasses out on the bed, pick them up pair by pair. I can't give them up, can't be that naked in the world, even for Gerry.

On Wednesday I dream Schroeder plays jazz on the piano and Snoopy dances, his big beagle ears flying out, his feet doing circles on the ground. He's still wearing his goggles and his smile stretches across his whole face. Charlie Brown reaches out and takes my glasses. He puts them in his pocket; he takes my hand. With our eyes closed, we begin to dance.

Trisha Hanifin

A version of this work was published in *Flash Frontier* (July 2014).

The moon in a bowl of water

Mother said, in the Old Country you make a lot of kids, they're money in the bank, water in the bucket. And you give them names taken from the Good Book. And still, you know so many of them are going to die before they're ready to fly; you hardly have time to shake a fist to heaven. And she dressed in permanent black.

In the New Country, Father replied, you have as few kids as possible, or none; and you might end up living almost forever in a small, fat town where your neighbours always shout hello and never goodbye, and their motor-mowers are so proper they hardly make a sound, they whisper.

Because we were running out of words to tell love and I didn't know what to say, I said: 'That dog of time is already on a short leash, barking at the traffic, biting the air and the moon in a bowl of water. And you know, the banks have turned into penny arcades. Not a single safe-deposit box hosting the tongues of strangers like ourselves. And the jackpot, if ever you get around to it: a leap year's supply of fortune-cookies.'

Michael Harlow

A version of this work was published in *Flash Frontier* (August 2016).

After the neighbours disappear

Like a last snow moon, the neighbours disappear. Homes – ghosted hulks carried aloft Kenworths – vanish to places called elsewhere. Abandoned, the Orphan family peer through thin glass at the sea's silver halo. The house rocks in late wind as if the Orphans are aboard a boat. Darkness plays out their isolation as a soundtrack: Cole Porter, DeBarge, Corona, Bastille …

Tomorrow, the Orphans will inhabit a future built of auctions and shark-nosed cars hunting their street. But presently, they dance along broken pavements, the kids play across empty land. And each night, they sink towards slumber, the sea creeping closer, closer ...

Siobhan Harvey

This work was previously published in *Flash Frontier* (December 2015).

Borrowing Anne Sexton's attire

I'm thinking of a black dress.

I'm thinking of nakedness.

I'm thinking of becoming an Anne Sexton wannabe who, like a white-trash Marilyn clone, reminds the world of how dead skin is shed as ruthlessly as a poet discarding words for the sake of the rhyme.

I'm thinking of a song, of 'The Ballad of the Lonely Masturbator'. Serenading myself till twilight, I drink my whisky neat.

I'm thinking of feet and metre, of dactyls and trochaics, of a villanelle my friend Sylvia stole, the lament we shared.

I'm thinking of a woman's voice, of bitterness calloused by bad choices, bad marriages and bad men.

I'm thinking of a tour, of readings where I wear a red gown and nothing underneath. My cigarette half-cocked, I listen to an inner voice, tender as a girl's, persuading me to soften my delivery.

I'm thinking of the children I never bore.

I'm thinking of letting go. Not an oven, but a closed garage and a car.

I'm thinking of the other side, of the paradise of having years trickle from my bones until old age has drained me, a borehole drawing off the sap.

I'm thinking of a Massachusetts Pine. Return me to it; bury me amongst its roots.

I'm thinking of a suit, skin-tight as a coffin or a collected works. *The Complete Poems*: an epitaph. Arriving home. No escape; the end.

SIOBHAN HARVEY

This work was previously published in *Lost Relatives* (Steele Roberts, 2011).

She and her first best boyfriend

The night before, all through the night before, she and her best first boyfriend are kneeling with their hearts literally held together, whole-heartedly happy. They are two open books placed carefully against each other so that the words shift and mingle to make two new stories.

DINAH HAWKEN

This work was previously published in *Small Stories of Devotion* (VUP, 1994).

I ate my brother

I ate my brother. I was always fond of him, looked up to him. He was older than me. I measured myself against him. We stood back to back. At first I only came up to his shoulder, and then I realised in that instant we'd fused.

It wasn't easy. He had to throw a coat over me so he could play with his friends. We'd bike off to the dark places children play. I'd be quiet so as not to cramp his style.

Then I began to grow and one morning, instead of him throwing a coat over me, I threw a coat over him and walked out the door.

I'd hear his voice in my ear sometimes. At first he wasn't impressed but he soon realised it was just easier this way, with me taking the lead. I was good at it.

As the years passed he became the size of a monkey on my back, an endearing, small lump, a strange surprise revealed to lovers. By the time I'd married and started having children he was the size of a pygmy marmoset.

The baby liked to play with him but eventually he became nothing but a calcified lump. A recent X-ray revealed three teeth and a shadow of fur.

HELEN HEATH

A version of this work was published in *4th Floor Literary Journal* (Whitireia Polytechnic, 2013).

To dislodge

1. Brace yourself

Forget about why he left you. Forget the whole last year. It never happened. Hit delete. Forget about your thinning skin and the grey that flecks your hair. Today your divorce is final. Today is the day everything will change. When people ask you how you're doing, tell them you're just fine. When your sister asks you out to dinner, don't make excuses. Take off the silver locket he'd had engraved with your initials. Tie your hair back with a ribbon. Put on some mascara. Go.

2. Hold tight

At dinner, make small talk with the waiter. Comment on the prawn cocktail. Ask about your nephew's job. When the couple at a nearby table coos and giggles, leaning close, smile quietly to yourself. Remember you got the house and the car and the cat. If you feel a tug of envy, take a sip of water. Think about your ex's bald spot. Think about his sweat-stained shirts. Picture him with his short-skirted tennis coach, her on top, his beer gut jiggling like unmoulded flan.

3. Pull free

Notice the tall man at the salad bar, between the olives and the tub of baby greens. Ask your sister if he smiled at you. Swear he did. Feel an ache crawl up from your belly and settle between your breasts. Leave your sister at the table. Say you need some air. Step out onto the verandah and lean against the railing. Remember how it feels to breathe.

Sally Houtman

This work was previously published in *Flash Frontier* (May 2012).

A mother's story

So strong is his will that it can produce a simulacrum of patience, prudence and fortitude at those moments when he feels most exposed, fragile and erratic. The stronger his attraction the more extreme his reaction, so the closer he is drawn the further he withdraws. Of course Nature does not acknowledge whatever's absent – it is prodigal with species, variations, effects – so any withdrawal is artificial, a perverse tearing of the Earth's fabric. This is how it appears to the West. Mahmoud knows that if a bird does not believe in trees it will not rest; he believes in the tree that is there yet, ultimately, he hopes to rest in the tree that is not there.

DAVID HOWARD

This work was previously published in *How to Occupy Our Selves* (HeadworX, 2003).

Dragonfly collage

The dragonfly's eyes are made up of multiple hexagons. Inside each hexagon is a black and white picture of my face. I've printed the photos from my files and glued them on, one by one. There must be at least a hundred. They're very small. You don't know they're faces until you look closely, then suddenly you see them, a million disembodied eyes staring at you in the dark.

Dragonflies are capable in darkness. I saw one in the hallway mirror after what I'd done. It involved a gun. No, it didn't. I like that *gun* rhymes with *done*. A knife. I took a knife outside and sliced all the leaves off Mum's blood red begonias. You said that I should tell the truth. I am telling the truth, Alice. The begonias were the *first* thing I remember getting in trouble for. They're represented by one of my faces. My skill is this: to see everything from every direction simultaneously. I didn't want to take the Zyprexa. Though, at the time, I remembered thinking I don't have eight pairs of visual neurons like the dragonfly, yet I am capable of collating multiple parts into a whole, I will not be affected. I *said* I would take it. I think it's fair to say, *Alice*, that my stabbing of Mr Gotthard's cheek in front of three hundred and twenty-three spectators only deserves a small part of the picture.

Blunt craft scissors sharpen effectively on a raspy concrete floor. The dragonfly is very skilled. It tracks its prey, calculates its flight path and moves into it before you can blink. It must be a shock for the prey to see its own face reflected multiple times in the dragonfly's eye, don't you think?

Alice?

GAIL INGRAM

This work was previously published in *Flash Frontier* (August 2016).

Whispers

A rabbit pops out of a hole. A mangy hare, in fact, her eyes glassy, looking for escape.

She has six kits in the warren below. Their fur is mangy too, stiff. Death is on her tongue, a taste that seems to come from inside, rather than, say, some poisoned carrot, blanched like the landscape.

The wind catches the willows out left. There. She bounds from the dust-bowl entrance. Darts left, right, her gait uneven. Stops as suddenly as she began. Here. Her coat blends tan-grey into tussock. Her nose quivers, for the first time, her eyes look interested.

Dark clouds press the horizon. A rumble. The hills look closer. Watch. They open like a walnut-shell cracks. And the ground, where the hare sits, blows like breath.

The horizon has split. Two nut-halves. Lightning crackles between the broken hill. A crack begins to run across the earth towards the hare. Her whole being shifts towards it; her ears lean into it, she trembles. The crack has singular direction, and tussock, stone, tree fall into its wake.

It travels more quickly than you think. She reacts now. Uses her hind legs to propel herself. For a moment she is high above the crack. Her fur is no longer dull but sleek, her front-legs reach skyward, she is in motion.

We can remember her like this. We don't need to imagine the rush downwards towards the open earth into crumbling, bone-crunching mineral. Let us recall her fine last leap towards her kittens.

GAIL INGRAM

This work was previously published in *Flash Frontier* (February 2015).

Dreaming of a desert rose

Disorienting. In her books the colours of the night are always blue. But the light filtering through the tree branches is grubby orange.

There is an odd scent in the air. Arid. Reminds her of old manuscripts and the tang she felt behind her eyes reading about the fate of Pompeii. The ancient impressions of bodies and ash.

She'd been thinking of the desert. She'd picked a rose. She –

– she didn't usually go out into the garden at night. Dew gummed her socks between her toes. Was there meaning in the clumsy handling of the kitchen scissors in her left hand? She stood by the apricot rose her mother had owned. Mist agglutinated around the streetlight, a Vesuvian eye.

She'd put it in the kitchen drawer to dry. *Certainly, she always pressed her flowers. It made them ancient. And tired.*

She must go to bed.

At the foot of the stairs, she notices her feet are wet. And the smell. Rubbing locked knees, she retraces her shuffled footprints.

Thick plumes cascade ceilingwards, threading from the door of the oven. From lumbersome to lunging, her hands find their way to the handle, then violently withdraw. The oven trembles as if it were laughing, lecherous orange teeth gnarring from behind the haze.

It's awfully dark, and hot. Her lungs hack. Perhaps she is dreaming of Pompeii again.

She doesn't associate roses and ovens until the fire alarm goes off.

Rata Ingram

The roadkill witch

Wendy was out wearing her high-vis vest before the morning traffic started. In winter she wore the cap with LED lights, much more practical than carrying a torch. But it was almost November and all she needed was a spade.

The first casualty she came across had a thick pelt, a crushed skull, and little white fingers splayed and stiff. Dried blood stuck the head to the tarmac. Using the spade, she gently loosened that contact and slid the blade under the body. She carried it to the side of the road.

'We'll find a nice spot for you.'

The soil was easy. She lined the trench with the thick, glossy leaves and the blue flowers of vinca growing in the ditch. She lowered the body with care and covered it, smoothing the surface.

'Rest in peace.'

The dead were a rabbit with a damaged hind leg, two more possums and a cat with a broken back. The poor mite was skin and bone, with the rusty brown fur of the local ferals.

Wendy stood up and eased her back. A car swerved fast round the corner, music blaring, lads yahooing.

'It's that roadkill witch.'

She didn't hear the jeers, see the finger. A cataclysmic event was happening in her chest.

The ambulance driver, without local knowledge, followed his satnav. He took the metal road with its steep inclines, sudden dips, potholes, shoals of gravel on the bends. Wendy's bones were shaken and shaken.

The hospital was noisy, the lights glaring. A nurse tried to put a line in a 'wandering vein'. When Wendy was left with the beeping monitors, the drips dripping, the tubes in her nose, she closed her eyes and conjured up soft, dark earth, mosses and the drifting scent of jasmine.

KAMALA JACKSON

Yesterday

Yesterday stayed open stretching itself without inhibition into all the days that followed the quake.

I hadn't the strength to close it; neither, it seemed, had anyone else.

When yesterday embraced me with its loneliness I made my mihi, my ancient greeting, and we wrapped ourselves around each other lost in a sea of consolation.

I built a boat, asked yesterday to accompany me.

We rowed in silence towards the shoreline where tomorrow waited.

Teoti Jardine

This work was previously published in *Flash Frontier* (December 2016).

The possum hunt

Yesterday, my tree was heavy with the suede softness of peaches.

Last night you feasted, leaving only corrugated husks and tattered flesh on the ground. Somewhere you are folded around your swollen belly.

Now, I hunt. The bush sheds the dappled light of day and fades to moonshine-deep. Soon the night will come. I am wrapped in the warp and weft of dusky shadows, tracing the threads of your passage from one totara to another. My shoes are as silent as whispers. The grizzled silver ferns brush me lightly as I pass – dew-drizzled ghosts in the billowing mist of my breath.

Steaming pellets rest lightly on the leaf litter; a scatological signpost pointing north-east, and the dubstep of my heart trips into triple step. The scent of musk settles under the weight of my attention: heavy, gamy.

I am still; the bullets are restless.

JAC JENKINS

This work was previously published in *Flash Frontier* (July 2012).

Pink light catches my eye

Pink light catches my eye. A building the size of a cathedral. Huge doorways. Three trains inside. From the top of ladders little men in white overalls lean over them, touch them. It looks as though the men are rubbing the trains down, the way old men used to rub rugby players with liniment before a game, but maybe the men are patting them. They could even be scraping something off the skin, as with barnacles on the hull of a ship.

Four or five others are sitting a little way back from the entrance, at an angle, waiting. Trains are like this with each other; tactful, and patient. For them, space is never assumed. It is occupied, or relinquished according to a Mandarin sense of entitlement.

Maybe pink light shining through the huge doorways at both ends of the building is their equivalent of the yellow glow we hope to see in the windows when we come home in the dark? That feeling that someone knows how hard the day has been, and has prepared a fire for us to sit by?

I want to be that man in white overalls on the top step of a ladder. I would rub their skin with soft cloths and grease. I would know them all by number. I would never criticise them for a little crustiness, or a crotchety outburst.

I want to absorb pink light, and then absorb more, until every cell in my body radiates light. Pink light my body. My body pink light.

LYNN JENNER

This work was previously published in *Dear Sweet Harry* (AUP, 2010).

It starts before the drinking

It starts before the drinking. Let's sidle up to him and sit with him at the bar. The bartender is rolling her eyes because now he is telling her how life isn't fair. She's wearing a blue dress as tight as a condom. Her lips remind him of the gash of pink highlighter on an overdue invoice. He distracts himself by scratching at the film of old liquor on the bar with the gnawed-down nail of his index finger.

In his car the wheels break up the salt on the road, like a stent in a bad artery. He puts on some country and western music. The bartender sings along. Her voice is too high for Johnny Cash.

At the motel he doesn't know where to hang his hope. There aren't any coat hangers. There isn't a hook on the back of the bathroom door.

They curl on the bed and when he gets out his wallet she says his daughter is beautiful. She gets out a picture of her own kid. She's stolen some whisky from the bar. It's the cheap stuff. It's yellow as a cat's eye. When she passes out in his arms he is both fascinated and afraid for her. In sleep you are open to all memories. He finishes the bottle. When it's not enough, he drinks the Listerine she's brought in her toiletries bag and posts the empty bottle out the crack in the bathroom window.

Elysia Rose Jenson

This work was previously published in *Flash Frontier* (September 2014).

Connections: a New Zealand novel in 224 words

Ake used to eel in Ōhāriu where his hīnaki got so full it dragged him under.

John, from Eketāhuna, sells insurance. He's trying to be a city slicker.

Lily rows her clinker on the Mahurangi harbour, and laments the urban creep to its shores.

Jemima suffers from premature menopause – lost all the babies she never had, her friends indelicately remind her.

Garry drives a truck; takes pills to stay awake and pills to sleep.

Brendan sleeps under a bridge and turns tricks for repressed men.

Tanya flies model planes because her dad won't let her study to be a pilot like he was.

All of these people are connected.

Ake, after his near-death experience, moved to Auckland and slept rough, and goes by the name of Brendan.

Brendan gave Garry a blowjob in Galatos Street, behind K Road.

Jemima, childless, is married to John – who desperately wants kids, and is having an affair with Tanya, and plans to leave Jemima one day when he plucks up the courage (which he has never possessed). They built a bach at Mahurangi West with all the money they saved by not having to feed and clothe and educate another human.

It is Jemima's bach in particular that Lily despises, with its stainless steel railings all the way down the ostentatious boat ramp to the water's edge.

D. R. Jones

A version of this work was published in *Landfall 229* (Autumn 2015).

What we built

Every city is a hymn to the wind, and the wind is rising. Remove the roofs and doors, peel back the cladding. Feel the breeze enter, plucking the strings of wire and cable, heralding the melody.

Every city is an opportunity for music: the rhapsody of meetings, the trilling of mobile phones, the timpani of falling concrete. The traffic stalls: let the ground bass fall silent. In the realm of fire and air, the upper voices play.

Do not let the wind shriek so and bend itself about. Placate it with offerings: the topmost tiers of stadiums, houses reverting to wood and iron, a single, startled flying cow. A threnody of uprooted trees.

When the storm has passed, look to the roofs. Some among you will want to replace them, to build again. Reconsider. Let your cities, unroofed and empty, sing the wind's long song.

Tim Jones

This work was previously published in *New Sea Land* (Submarine imprint, Mākaro Press, 2016).

Secondhand palm

Lord, those gangs. New Orleans crawls with 'em. They're always thieving from me. And what're they gonna do with my goods? Sell them on the streets? Nah. Who'd pay for 'em? I think they're giving my goods to their grandmas. Yes, sir. I just want a house with iron balconies and hanging baskets filled with ferns and pretty flowers in baskets on the railing. Orleans style. But those gangs, Lord. The police aren't bothered. But they're thieving from me! Pulling the goods right out of my baskets. Roots and all.

I found evidence of the thieving once. Followed a trail of pink impatiens petals from the empty baskets on my porch, across my driveway, to the neighbour's driveway. That's where the getaway car parked. That's where the petals stopped. I got down on my knees to look close to make sure. Could've yelled, 'Stop! Hooligans!' but they were long since gone.

Even after the storm the thieving didn't stop. Storm left nothing of my house but rubble and ashes and my *one palm tree*. And someone came along and stole my one palm tree when I was holed up with my sister in the Quarter. Lost everything else but that tree. Family pictures. Mama's recipes. Pop's records. Tree hadn't been in the ground more than a month and what's that gang gonna do with a secondhand palm tree? Brighten their grandma's hurricane-wrecked house? Damn horticulture gangs. The police got bigger things to think about.

They're busy thieving stuff themselves.

Brindi Joy

A version of this work was published in *Flash Frontier* (July 2013).

Red sea

There was a red sea on his knee with scalloped skin shores. I was impressed by the brightness of it – how much white glinted in the sun, maybe because his knee was bent. He was riding on the overbridge where Oakley Creek passes into the mangroves that become Point Chev beach. That's where the escapees from Carrington would run and hide and wait, we'd say, because they wouldn't know what to do next. *Don't look down there for too long because you might see someone or they might see you.* He straddled his red bike jauntily. The sun was too hot, his skin flickering wet brown. He was weaving, the handlebars twisting the wrong way. I felt like I shouldn't be watching. *Go home*, someone yelled, or *Come with me*.

Simone Kaho

This work was published in *Lucky Punch* (Anahera Press, 2016).

Waterfall

We were nine when Henry said he wished he could start his life over. I asked him *why*. We were at Oakley Creek looking at the waterfall; water from the top tipping into the water below, filling and refilling the stone-ringed pool. There was a neighbourhood legend that a kid had died jumping off the waterfall one summer. It could've been made up. The stories say that he hit his head on a stone or his foot got stuck at the bottom of the pool and he drowned. *I've done too many bad things,* Henry said. *It's too late for me. No,* I said, *only grown-ups have to say that.* I wanted to tell him I was sad too – about our walk being over when he finished looking at the waterfall.

Simone Kaho

This work was previously published in *Lucky Punch* (Anahera Press, 2016).

The great race

We lined them up at the starting post, re-positioned them so that at least they were facing the right way. Albie drew a finish line in marker pen a ruler's length away.

Mine was the one with the red spot on its shell – painted carefully, mindful of the shell's fragility. Albie painted his striped. And he called it Stewie, though it didn't need a name.

And they were off. We cheered for them, for every hard-won millimetre. We promised them luxury prizes: fast cars, overseas holidays, the affections of beautiful snail-women.

Albie was a head shorter than the rest of us – shortest kid in class. Glasses. Curly hair. A protruding bottom lip. He had this way of staring at people – not really at them but through them, as if he had X-ray vision and could beam it straight for their souls. When he talked at all it was something random, something nobody else got. No wonder then that he had trouble with other kids.

But I liked being his one friend. It made us part of a club that only we belonged to.

'He's just shy,' my mother said, but I knew there was more she didn't want to say.

Approaching the finish line, he lifted Stewie up off the racetrack and lay him on my forearm.

'He concedes,' Albie said brightly. 'Johnno' – the name he'd given my snail – 'reigns victorious.'

He was a weird kid.

Rosalie Kempthorne

A version of this work was published in *Flash Frontier* (April 2016).

The Parable of the Beans

Shipwrecked, you wash up on the island on a large pallet of tinned beans. Congratulations, you salt-blessed good-lucker. But it turns out that bashing open a tin of beans with a rock burns precisely the same number of calories found in the tin – 159 in a 200-gram serve. I don't know why: tough tins and an impish metabolism, I guess. So you do the needful labour non-stop for weeks, bringing tin to rock and rock to tin, your arm vibrating like a cracked cricket bat. 'This is living,' you say to yourself, living. You get to the last tin, and you are still unrescued, regarded warily by the uncatchable petrels, mocked by distant whale-spouts. You untwist the ridged, mangled metal. Inside is a business card: 'You could already be done by now if you'd called Central Pacific Tin-Bashers.' The sea is flat and the salt stains on your trousers make marvellous rings.

Erik Kennedy

Just my luck

Just Mum's luck to end up with Mad Rowdy. She reckons she's cursed when it comes to relationships, not that she believes in God. I do. I was keepin' out of Rowdy's way last Saturday, when I saw Jesus. I'd just scored a half-eaten burger from the bin outside of Maccas. I dropped the wrapper and it blowed down the street and got stuck on his leg. He was stood in the Square on a box. The shoppers, all wearing puffer jackets, pushed their hands deep into their pockets and pretended to look in the shop windows when they passed him.

Jesus' arms stretched out from his sides. His fingers bent up, like he was weighing the clouds. And here's the best bit: he was starkers, 'cept for a white towel around his privates. Yeh, and he had this kind of spiky ring on his head.

I went for a closer look. He was standing real still. He wasn't even blinking. His brown eyes were kind of wild and he had big bushy eyebrows. The tin can in front of his box sat on a square of red fabric held down at each corner by rocks. I checked the tin for cash. It was empty.

'Hi, Jesus,' I says. 'Think it's going to rain?'

He nodded.

A passing bull terrier pissed against his box. The yellow stream soaked into the cloth and made a stain around his tin. Jesus stared up to Heaven: just his luck.

I got soaked going home, so I copped it big time. I'm going to see Jesus again next Saturday. Need to ask him what I can do about Rowdy.

Sue Kingham

This work was previously published in *Flash Frontier* (July 2014).

Salt

My father called us a tribe of savages and perhaps in our souls we still are. Barefoot, barely tamed, the half-dozen children of a Waikato dairy farmer with Presbyterian habits and peppery temper. We were restless and rowdy, muted in church by barley sugars passed along the pew from Mum's navy purse.

He was a clock prisoner, my father, chained to routine. His 5:00am alarm reverberated through our childhood, dragging us from our dreams to dully register the backdoor slam, the metronome of gumboots quick-marching into dawn.

Our house was draughty, wooden, starved of sunlight by a circle of pines. Mould sprouted in wardrobes, wetas nested under beds, and winter lingered like an old man who won't be budged. Icy mornings, my siblings and I jostled to dress in front of the smoking wetback.

Porridge, prized for its three-ingredient economy, was breakfast year-round. Mum blobbed it into bowls and we'd sit waiting for our father to come in from milking, wearing smells of dung and hay. Always efficient, he ate his porridge in six large spoonfuls, silently.

Only one morning was different: my mother was bedridden with bronchitis; she croaked breakfast-making instructions to us. The result, after fierce squabbling, was black-flecked glue. We smeared it into bowls and waited for our father. He sat, took his first mouthful, grimaced, put down his spoon, and cleared his throat.

'Porridge is *three* ingredients,' he said.

He stood and picked up the glass saltcellar with his chafed-red hands. Working his way around the table, he leaned over, sprinkling and stirring smidgeons of salt into each plate. His rough fingers balanced the tiny silver spoon delicately between index and thumb. Wordless, we watched him, the air thrumming with a great pity that felt like love.

LYNNE KOHEN

This work was previously published in *Flash Frontier* (August 2016).

Book of clouds

Cirrus
He sat on a chair on the strip of lawn below the washing line. The ground sloped towards the steps and the wind yawned. I walked around him. Crouched. Stood back. I snipped at his curls again and again.

Nimbostratus
On our way home from quiz night, we flew through the tunnel, shouting out Smiths lyrics: *happy in the haze of a drunken hour*. It wasn't until we entered the open silence of the other side that we felt foolish. We walked quietly until Cuba Street.

Stratocumulus
I'm wearing polyprop in bed. Two feather duvets, a cheap one and a patchwork quilt on top. I push my numb feet under his and claim a lumpy pile of pillows.

Mammatus
Jo starts her treatment next week, so on Friday night we all met her at the pub. She handed out pink ribbons to everyone she knew and wore a set of flashing boobs on her head. It was like a hen's party. Except she broke up with her partner last month.

Contrails
After the visitors left, beard trimmings seasoned the soap. Deep-sleep smells were folded into the couch and pots were lost for days. A note of thanks lay on the bench with an apology for using all the dishwashing liquid.

Pileus
Three young men emerged from the community arts centre, their creative minds kept under tight beanies. Inside, a light flickered across a row of windows. We stopped for a moment to watch. Was this an installation to be admired, or faulty wiring in need of funding?

SARADHA KOIRALA

This work was previously published in *Wit of the Staircase* (Steele Roberts, 2009).

Yard duty

I'm teaching again. Students smile at me and say hi as we pass in the corridor. Sometimes they ask how I am. When we're practising writing they say, 'What's the name of that feeling like butterflies in your stomach, but not excitement?' 'Anxiety,' I tell them. 'Anxiousness,' they say.

On Monday and Wednesday lunchtimes I'm on yard duty. I have to shoo the students out of the corridors and I have a walky-talky that I assume works, but have never used, except to pretend to call for back-up when someone asks too much of me. I hold it near my mouth and make a fake static noise. Kkkkkk. They get the idea. Move on.

Today a bird was trapped inside. There was a warm breeze and the sun was out, but that bird was obsessed with the unopenable window at the top of the stairs; wouldn't move from the windowsill, fluttered its wings like the butterflies in our stomachs, oblivious to the door we'd opened at the end of the empty hall.

Saradha Koirala

So things end

He straightened himself on the hoe and saw the vortices of dust on his very far left down on the road towed behind the black, square Hummer. Of all that there was to be seen – the crisp peaks and screes, the river in its silvery, molten gorge to the right and the green, clouded, undulating hills to the north – vanished into the background of this tiny movement. He thought again about the way in which everything could be occluded for the sake of what mattered, how you could focus on the cello in a string quartet and hear it and not the two violins and viola, how the captain of a frigate could ignore the sight of a keelhauled man and command his barnacle-scarified corpse thrown back into the water for the sharks, for the sake of maintaining order.

It was time.

Koenraad Kuiper

Beggars, choosers

Maurice Oliver, 83, was hot and tired. But walking wasn't something he was going to give up. It was good for him, everyone said so.

As the street steepened, Maurice thought about something that had disturbed him earlier today, in Queen Street. Beggars, sitting on the footpath, on pieces of cardboard, placards propped up in front of them, bearing pathetic, misspelt messages. 'Bus fair?' 'Havnet eaten for days.' One young woman's read, 'Sexualy Abussed'. The beggars all had upturned caps or cups beside them, in which were a few miserable coins.

Many of these mendicants were young, and didn't look in any way disabled. What they had in common was a glassy-eyed listlessness. He had ignored their importuning cards, caps and cups. They disgusted him.

A bus swished past, giving off a gust of air which almost blew Maurice's hat off. He clutched it. It was an old panama, crumpled and stained, but one that he was fond of.

The road became steeper. Maurice felt short of breath, and his shirt was damp under the arms.

Maurice stopped, undid the top buttons of his shirt and loosened its collar. Further on was a wooden seat. He dropped down onto it. Relief. He fanned his face with his hat, then placed it, crown down, on the seat beside him.

Lying back, he closed his eyes. His head slumped. In seconds he was asleep.

A truck roared past. Maurice woke with a start. Where was he? What time? He looked at his watch. One-thirty. Good grief, he'd been out for an hour. Falling asleep on a street bench, what must people have thought?

Maurice looked down. His hat was still there. And in it were two twenty cent coins and a single golden dollar.

GRAEME LAY

A version of this work was published in *The New Zealand Listener* (20 February 2017).

Drawing

You know I was really good at art. I showed early promise. I was always drawing and people said how good it was, and they thought I was so good, they tried to make me make a life of it that I didn't want – so much that they didn't listen when I said I want to drop out of art school. And they pushed and bullied and I sat silent then cracked and tore off my clothes and ran screeching down the street with all the neighbours watching; my father running, tackling me down as if I were a rugby ball, dragging me back, with my knees and palms and elbows full of gravel and bleeding.

And when I got ill many years later, I would draw on a little A4 pad to calm myself so I might fall asleep, and the drawings I did, I did not get praise for. I was purposely naive and thinking of nothing when I drew, which was something different. As a child might do in the privacy of its world. A world of no fridge magnets, and never having to show anyone.

Wes Lee

To die and die again

I die and die again. Smoke a cigarette, watch my body roll into the road then vanish under the wheels of a truck. To get up and do it all over.

And the night is black and the page is black, there is no blank page, just tomorrow and tomorrow, waiting for the wormhole to do its work (where I disappear).

I must like suffering you said, to do it. I must like suffering I tell myself. Renewal, the body in the road, the woman made perfect, the woman made whole, scooped back into the blue dress and shining.

And sometimes I'm the detective, the gumshoe locking his brown office with the vague, knobbled window (in the heavy oak door). His narrow eyes, the tough set of his mouth.

And sometimes I am paint around a body with the rain so sleety (the dumpster's handiness).

And sometimes I am a street with no lights that only the drunk or stoned would walk down.

A searchlight from a helicopter.

WES LEE

A version of this work was published in *Landfall 233* (Autumn 2017).

They are out on the point

They are out on the point having a quiet beer in the dark, the young men who grew up here and like to revisit old haunts. The moon is up, the evening is calm and free. Boats row out of the harbour with wings of fire. A door opens and a crowd of old people pours across the road down the steps and into the sea whooping and hollering. How old? I ask. Very old, he says, the young man who is telling the story. They were ocean swimmers on a midnight training run following the path of the moon towards North Head. He swears they were every one of them naked. Not that you could see much. But it makes a change from the parrot man and his two companions in their large hats. Or the woman in her sackcloth rummaging the bins at night with old Charlie. Or Walkie Talkie striding the pavements ceaselessly, once in a hoodie they were too scared to reclaim. Or the woman in tulle pushing her pram about the streets when they were little, her daughters dressed as fairies. The stencilled monarch butterflies that appeared in bus shelters and on walls one night when nobody was looking. The pink and purple house. The salt devils. The wooden toys and the palm-tree mugs sitting on the kitchen hatch. This evening a pack of Sea Scouts is rafting up in the waves, shrill voices of children scrambling from one kayak to the next then it all falls apart as someone goes into the water. Shrieks of delight from the other side. This morning one of the float planes is taxiing across the harbour beside us, then the pilot opens the throttle and it takes off into the light breeze from the south.

Michele Leggott

This work was previously published in *Vanishing Points* (AUP, 2017).

We know what the dog of tears will do next

We know what the dog of tears will do next, he who has been trailing the woman standing on the balcony looking up at the sky. She is the woman who wept, he is the dog who licked away her tears. They have gone on like this for some time, the only woman who can see and the dog who is now more human than he wants to be. His nails scratch the wooden floor. His belly is as empty as everyone else's but he does not mind. He is walking towards the woman on the balcony. When he reaches her she will bring her eyes down to look at the ruined city and become blind. Everyone else will have their eyes back. She will have the dog of tears. The dog will bark holes in the last page of the book and lead her through one of them. There they are, the dog of tears and the woman who wept. His nails click on the rough stones. She who can no longer see begins to tell a story. They pass the street of crocodiles, the pool of tears, the hill of forty days and the hill of forty nights. They pass the little seahorse in its salty pool. They pass a white rose, a black swan, a blue biddy. The dog kills another hen and they roast it over a small fire. They can hear the sea, its fronding on smooth sand, its talking against rocks, its clapotis bouncing off stone walls. What might we not do with the hot bones dripping fat, she says. Two birds rise into the air on wings the colour of ash. Did you hear that she asks the dog licking away the salt on her cheeks.

Michele Leggott

This work was previously published in *Vanishing Points* (AUP, 2017).

On the road

Road trip

On the road to prison, they met three hitchhikers.

The first was lying on the verge under a sheet. They got a helluva fright when he sat up and said, 'Taihape?'

The second had a cardboard sign on which was written, 'HARMLESS!' They doubled back, when they were done laughing, to get him. He was very cheerful – and Japanese – but not for long. They left him on Vinegar Hill, where they stopped for the view, a piss, and more pills.

The third had an American accent and great legs. When she, too, stopped breathing, they were nearly there.

Long shadows

So Jody and I were scuffing along in our jandals, towels round our necks, when a car stopped beside us and the driver, a mum-aged woman bawling her eyes out, asked us the way to the cemetery. We sent her up the hill, and from the beach we could see her there, all day, slumped by a praying angel overlooking the bay. It pissed us off. First day of the holidays, all we wanted to do was bask like pumpkins and talk shit, and all we could feel was her shadow.

FIONA LINCOLN

'Road trip' was previously published in *Flash Frontier* (December 2016).
'Long shadows' was previously published in *Flash Frontier* (December 2015).

The true story

Jack:

I walked with Jill, up the hill, with high hopes, swinging my pail. I had in mind to try again for a kiss. In school and in dreams, I think of nothing but her red lips, her plump arms, her red lips. I know her mum won't mind, who calls me Dear, feeds me cake, and tries to get me in the barn alone. Her younger sisters, one-two-three, think me a dish – *Oh, Jack*, they say, *Oh! Jack!* – but Jill's scowl, it lights me up like firecrackers.

Up ahead, in scarlet shorts, her haunches whisper back and forth like bold, beckoning fingers. I think she will say yes.

The sun is hot. My thirst is sharp. I lick my lips. We're nearly there.

*

Jill:

My stupid father made me come. He's holding a fistful of daughters like batons to relay, and Jack in his sights a likely runner. Stupid Jack, who charms my mum and sisters with his greasy swagger.

Here's the well. Jack's given me the pail, the better to watch me bend over. I feel his hand on my bottom and come up swinging. CRACK, the bucket hits his head. THUD, he falls.

Guilt makes me kneel to look.

The dent in his head steals my breath.

A pulse at his throat gives me hope.

His face, relaxed, belongs to a different boy.

I see who he could be.

When time resumes, he's woken up. The swagger's back, but it's too late. Fuck. I've fallen for him. And he knows it.

FIONA LINCOLN

Scheherazade

In the bar, my lover is silent. He acts bored and says he is tired. I see him glance around the bar as if in search of better company.

I tell him this story I read in a newspaper. A man in China went to a hospital complaining of complications from surgery. The doctors found nothing wrong, but the man refused to leave his bed.

After a year, a new chief of staff took over the hospital. He said the man had to be removed. It took six policemen to carry him out. On a stretcher. He was still wearing his pyjamas, I tell my lover.

My lover blinks. He casts a covert glance at me as if possibly he may have a question or two in his mind.

I do not wait for him to speak. I begin another story.

Kate Mahony

The youth in the park

I relax on the park bench. He sits on the wooden seat, looks at me. 'Hello.' 'Hello,' I reply. I'm watching my granddaughters. 'Aren't they old enough to take care of themselves?' he asks. He has interesting eyes, one brown, one blue. His blue eye is droopy, the lashes at half-mast. I say that once it might have been safe but it's risky today.

One of the girls flings herself on me. 'You're base,' she says.

He comes from Te Kuiti. 'Farmers?' I ask. He smiles at me with his uneven eyes. He says he will return to Te Kuiti when the sun goes down.

I need to stretch and I walk over to the swings where the girls are poking their skinny legs through the late afternoon sunlight. He follows and tells them how lucky they are to have such a cool grandmother. They invite him to play a game of tiggy. He hasn't played for years but is a good soccer player and has sharp footwork. The girls disappear inside the castle but in a moment he is with me again. There is a nip in the air. Beyond the dunes the waves crash on the shore.

autumn afternoon
the girls race to me
I am base again

Catherine Mair

A version of this work was published in Catherine Mair and Patricia Prime, *Morning Glory* (2006).

Fahrenheit

That was the autumn my father died. His dying involved long and then longer visits to the hospice, plus the unlikely presence of my brother and sister. They had flown in from their particular foreign cities but chose to stay in a local hotel, taking turns to complain about the heat. Weirdly, what I remember most from that time is the morning I noticed the new neighbour staring over the fence. It was early in the day, and he stood there a long time. He seemed to be looking towards my house but also far into the distance. When I went over, he introduced himself as Dr Fahrenheit, and told me, by way of explaining his gaze, that he was hoping to catch sight of his wife, who had, as he put it, 'wandered off'. It was a strange encounter, and we never progressed beyond those first, awkward civilities. If the wife existed, I never saw her. Now a young family lives next door. Sometimes a ball will appear on the lawn and a small boy comes round to fetch it. As for Dr Fahrenheit, over the years since our brief exchange I have formulated several clumsy jokes, all to do with temperature, and have always felt pleased that I did not make them.

Bill Manhire

This work was previously published in *Some Things to Place in a Coffin* (VUP, 2017).

Pig song

The man carrying the pig out of the bush hopes it is dead pig. It stumbles with him, it is big on his back. Towards nightfall it grows innards, grows more of itself, blood and guts, shows teeth and tusks and the dead dogs on its tusks, and it calls to the man, sings to him, a little song then a big song, a squeal of song then a grunt, *chanson*, listening hard in the dark, and so all the way home to the crackling.

Bill Manhire

January in Ireland

She's all grown up now. All trussed up like a Tudor feast.

At her dad's funeral (she didn't know him well) his brother came over and said *Sorry for your loss, love.* And then, swallowing first, *Jaysus, you're huge, you've gone huge.*

He said huge with two syllables. *Hew-age.*

His eyes fixed on her buttercream breasts. Luscious and richly spilling out of black lace, a corset worn tightly laced by itself, pushed up over a pale plump belly. Tender as dough rising over torn velvet shorts.

January in Ireland is not the weather for shorts. She hasn't the legs either. Even with those fuck-you heels.

But she doesn't care about all that.

She's proud of herself whatever she is. She knows the power of youth though she doesn't yet know she knows.

And so we laughed, my sister and I. Really laughed and were glad of it all. Comedy and tragedy. A right funeral. What else should we do?

She's all grown up now. *Hew-age.* And far from women who apologise for themselves.

S. J. Mannion

A version of this work was published in *London Grip* (Winter 2016/17).

The patriots

When asked about Milford Sound, how it was and had I *ever seen*? Superlatives dismissed as overdone, I say, 'Oh, a real big deal, some chocolate box top, that. Ay?'

And in a final flourish, 'Stunning.'

Then, 'Yes, I have ever seen – being Irish. We are no strangers to beauty!' What I could have said, perhaps should have said, is:

Oh it is the gates of heaven.

A celestial cleft, a nave, a cathedral at large.

Waterfalls spume and column, spout and pour from altars of rock.

Pilgrim seals worship there, in sleek and monkish congregation.

It is a place to laugh, to weep, to wish to live or to die there.

Good just to be and be there. Good.

It is a prayer, fully realised, a sacred organ of the world.

A pulsing vein of arterial glory.

A direct line to God. Or No-God. To the stillness of all things, to the eternal movement.

But I didn't say that. That being a hard thing to say in a pub, with three drunk primary school teachers racking up the beers. Three proud lovers of their country and its particular glories. And sure – why wouldn't they be?

'This land has no monopoly on wonders, or beauty. Nor any land', I do say, somewhat foolishly, given the circumstances, the company, the fact that it was their round next.

And so, I was left to drink alone, in contemplation of language, its limits. Of loyalty.

S. J. Mannion

A version of this work was published in *Spectra Anthology* (Christchurch Writer's Guild, November/December 2016).

Not another nafanua poem

Not another nafanua poem she can hear them say as she attempts to ride the
current of her culture in the new millennium with her electric waka I'm afraid
so her shadow answers back in black but this ride's for nua's sister the one
who stayed home and fed her father koko alaisa wiping his chin and fetching
the key for the cupboard holding the toilet pepa for the faleuila outside while
her famous warrior sister slay the stereotypes on an oceanic scale I'm afraid so
because this is the story of how her sister had to replace the stolen coconuts
meant for that evening's saka that the warrior took without asking to cover her
womanhood I'm afraid so because someone had to feed the aiga harvest the
kalo the bananas the pawpaw bagging them and dragging them to makeke fou
to sell for kupe to pay the government school for the kids to get a scholarship
up and out of here so they can come back and open a restaurant in apia and
finally begin to tap into those rivulets of capitalism spilling over and into the
sewers and into the streets and into the back roads of the kua back villages
except for nafanua's village someone has to tell said the shadow.

Selina Tusitala Marsh

Author's note

Nafanua: ancient Samoan goddess of war, commonly mythologised, and renown for her battle prowess. She covered her breasts with coconuts and was believed to be a formidable male warrior until her womanhood was discovered.

Koko alaisa: a dish made from cooked rice, cocoa and sugar.

Faleuila: toilet.

Saka: boiled up dish (saka kalo is boiled taro).

Aiga: extended family.

Makeke fou: market place.

Kupe: money.

Kua back: villages 'at the back' or away from the more westernised (hence sophisticated) capital of Apia. Derogative in meaning.

This work was previously published in *Best New Zealand Poems 2006* (IIML, 2006).

Funeral in the rain

It is useless to resist the screenwriters' ubiquitous cliché, better to place an arm about its shoulder and guide the scene through the oh-so-familiar props. Black clad mourners beneath the weeping umbrellas, darkly sleek limousines slowing among the trees and graves. The sound of crows quite drowns out the ashes-to-ashes priestly monologue, and we note the widow's shapely ankles; a sister's lace handkerchief; stern, constrained colleagues with overcoat collars turned up; blue wild flowers clasped by a solemn child.

Then, at some remove, on misted, higher ground with tombstones, the solitary woman, austerely beautiful despite her grief, bowed as a question mark. Mistress, lover, long lost, or estranged, daughter, even avenger perhaps, who turns before the service ends and takes all eyes with her as she walks through the rain and the crows' mockery to the stone gates, and on farther into the plot.

Owen Marshall

Flies, heat

White as whey by the milk jug, the woman paddles pale hands through the liquid air, chasing flies. The orange heat of drought has brought them in. They hang in the heavy air, thunderous, or zipper the room to thud against windows. Such blundering, incessant, insistent knocking. Some, stunned, sit, fat Buddhas, on ledges. They clot like grapes on flypapers, or sucker on walls, rubbing wire legs together. They flex the omniscient bulbs of their eyes, confident, at ease. They paint the wide, white canvas of the ceiling with small pointillist dots. Some succumb to spray or swat. Dead flies heap on high shelves – their cellophane wings and crisped bodies a reminder of past parties, past mingling. Flies crawl on the muzzle of the brown dog that lies on the sun- swilled linoleum, the pink scarf of his tongue unfurling, unfurling. A cloud of flies drink the sweat on the woman's brow. She hates their threading tickle, their jostling for position. Now, the woman's arm is a tattoo of flies. Flies even ring the rim of the milk jug.

If only it would rain, she thinks.

STEPHANIE MAYNE

Dead space

Catch the boy out there standing like a bird with one foot tucked behind a calf looking at the sea. He isn't at soccer practice. He isn't on the Scout tramp to Chatham Creek. He isn't playing Dead Space 2 while Bridgie practices her scales. Up and down, up and down. The boy, Jesse, is allergic to scales and allergic to Bridgie who squeaks like a bird when he interrupts her. *Dead Space 2. Necromorphs, for God's sake. I need to concentrate.*

But she just squeaks and then she squeals and then Mum comes wiping her hands on a tea towel, and she wants to know where he got the damn game from. Then it's all over, Red Rover, as his dad says, and he's outside, like his dad usually is, smoking, except Jesse's not smoking because he's run out of smokes.

Catch the boy before he leaves. Not the boy leaving. The father leaving. Country Road bag in hand – Bridgie's bag for sleepovers. He says to the boy, 'Bye, Jess,' and he says to the boy, 'Be good for your mum.'

And his dad puts down the stupid bag, and the look on his face is that sort of look he gets when he comes home and it's his birthday and Mum's made a special dinner. Hopeful. Or something. *He blinks too much*, thinks Jesse, *his breath smells like shit*. When his dad hugs him, Jesse puts his foot down so he won't topple. The scales have stopped. Jesse thinks of Necromorphs. He smells sweat and smokes. *That's how Necromorphs would smell*, he thinks. *And they'd blink too fast*. His father used to play the piano. He bought the piano for Jesse to play but Jesse didn't want to play. He just didn't.

Mary McCallum

A version of this work was published in *Flash Frontier* (July 2013).

Leader of the pack

Jimmy Dog watches Nate – all smooth like he owns it – lifting the latch – sliding through – security guards wall-leaning – barely a glance – just like Ben minutes ago – all dressed up – smart – like entering work – but Jimmy Dog knows their game – 'coming-from-work-sneaking-into-a-festival' – he's more street style – a punter looking for a free entry point – but shit those dudes walked straight in – do it like that – like you own it – glances back at the sidewalk posse – Idaho, Harmony, Bones, Warchild – all waiting for his lead – be in character – just do it – now – takes his own cue – steps out – feeling self-conscious – crossing the road – hitting his stride – head up – chest out – guards haven't moved – up the kerb – over the sidewalk – body declaring I couldn't care less – reaching out for the gate – 'hey you' – they're coming over – 'yeah what' – blocking his way – 'you got ID' – facing up – 'I gotta be working man I'm late already' – 'you got ID' – 'lost it man but my boss has a new one for me' – 'nice try mate' – 'I'll go get it' – 'no ID no come through' – 'I'll bring it back to show you bro' – 'go to the main entrance and they can radio your boss' – 'I'm already late man' – guard points west – 'that's the only way you're coming in' – damn this feels like oppression – brown boys stomping on brown boys – but holds his cool – maintains character – 'damn you guys gonna get me in trouble I'm gonna be so late' – sidles off – the injustice stinging – even for a lie – gotta be another way – keep on circling – you'll find it – the chink in the armour – the hole in their wall – you always do – that's why they follow – the posse – doesn't bother looking back – knowing they're always there – watching – waiting turns – just a lag or two behind.

Allan McEvoy

This work was previously published in *North & South* (11 January 2017).

Crack

He was once a fisherman and used to own a dingy called *The Little Huia*. He'd catch kahawai and snapper, but throw the cod back. Never bought bait – pipi and mussels did the job.

She was once an English teacher, listened closely to the wind and drew pictures of cats while she talked on the phone.

He was shorter than most people, due in part to posture. Primary school was tough; he was an ugly duckling who grew into an ugly duck and learnt contentment.

She was all smokes, smiles and dribbling conversation. Had a face like leather and a heart like wool.

They were strangers, until a Tuesday afternoon, when they met on Main Street Otorohanga.

She was browsing the marigolds, outside the florist.

He was down on his luck and out for a stroll.

She decided to buy a few pots for the garden.

He decided to make off with a suitcase that an Armourguard employee had put down while refilling an ATM. It contained three thousand dollars.

She was heading up the street towards her '74 Kingswood, pots in hand.

He was sprinting down the street, aiming to lose his pursuers in the park.

She cracked him on the head with $12.98 worth of hardened clay; it was more on instinct than intent.

He crumpled to the pavement, like a scarecrow floored by a hurricane.

She apologised incessantly for her un-ladylike behaviour. The police officer could not stop laughing, while waving the ambulance on its way.

He awoke in Accident and Emergency, head pounding and craving a beer.

She was at his side. 'Are you okay? I didn't mean to hit you quite so hard.'

He didn't know what to say.

'Mary,' she said, offering her hand.

'Stan,' he said tentatively.

They shook hands.

Timothy McGiven

A version of this work was published in *Flash Frontier* (July 2012).

The huhu grub

Wiremu's superpower was being able to read people's minds. He had to tune in to their frequencies. This could take some time, especially when they held tightly to their secrets.

What people looked like on the outside had little to do with their inside thoughts. The old lady who sat on her peeling porch all day, for instance – he expected her to be thinking of nothing much. But her head was full of shrapnel and loud explosions and people running and crying. Mum said she was from somewhere far away.

Mum's head was full of slow static, tinged an ocean blue. Wiremu wanted to soothe her static, but he didn't know how. So he cleaned the house and helped feed his brothers and sisters and did all the dishes. Still her static seeped out of her eyes and her mouth and drenched everything with sadness.

At school, Wiremu's superpower helped him avoid the school bully. The bully thought in sharp rat-a-tats: *I'll catch that slow fat huhu grub today*. Black fury ricocheted out of the bully's mind and down the school hallways when Wiremu slipped away yet again.

'Class, we have a new girl today. Her name is Liseti. Please make her feel welcome.'

Liseti's eyes glittered, fierce and bird-like. Her hands clenched and unclenched. Wiremu wondered whether she would like him. Slow, chubby Wiremu, whom no one spoke to.

Liseti looked up sharply and stared straight at him. As if she had heard him.

Himali McInnes

A version of this work was published in *Flash Frontier* (April 2016).

Mountain

Stillness surrounds the Japanese lodge in the alpine pass. When she bows to it and becomes a mountain, her rented kimono learns to expand.

Leslie McKay

When gorillas sleep

I never touched the gorilla, I say. I got better things to do. Then the park ranger plonks his canvas bag on the table and pulls out a tranquiliser gun and we all stare at the gun and I know it will have my finger prints all over it and then he's saying, funny how you target the adolescent males, none of the silverbacks are shot, and I just about blurt out that's just chance, that is, but I hold my tongue and I'm thinking of fingerprints and even nose prints because each Ugandan gorilla has got its own, nobody else like it. *Listen up!* The park ranger bangs the table with his fist. A drop of sweat runs down his forehead. You think we're going to sit here, twiddle our thumbs while Rome burns? He leans forward, tells me the whole conservation programme is under threat, the government can pull its funding just like that and he's not going to see his job go down the tubes. *Listen up!*

I never touched the gorilla, I say. And then he tells me to think back to Lake Bunyonyi reserve yesterday afternoon and what was I doing there? He knows I was there, he has proof. Didn't I know there was cameras in the trees?

All the candelabra trees? I ask. I'm just stalling for time. I'm just stalling. I'm just. I stare out the window. The trees have red leaves shaped like hearts.

You ever laid your hand on a gorilla's chest? You ever felt the warmth of wiry hair, the roughness under your palm? Ever lain down with your brother, your ear listening to his heart beat?

Frankie McMillan

A version of this work was published in *New Flash Fiction Review* (2016).

In the weekend we went to the beach

The beach isn't that great without the sun. Dad said as much, but Mum insisted we stick to the plan. We all must suffer for his misdeeds. A fish-skin sky draped over the sea.

I dutifully arranged shells and thin bones around her while he, with false cheer, incited the building of a sandcastle. He called her his queen but she was merciless. I dodged beneath the contracted moments where they looked past each other.

Seawater surged into unguarded moats. She sighed. It sounded like pain. The waves placed scales of salt on my shins.

We walked to the car, weighed down with damp towels, and bags, and a hefty silence we knew wouldn't stay clammed up forever. A thick line was drawn where the ocean and sky could find no compromise.

He dropped a towel, almost on purpose. The accusations spat out of her. He snapped back. I saw my chance to dash through the space between them, back to the edge to kick at tractor waves churning dark sand. I lifted my eyes. The cloud-scales had tugged loose and the sky was cluttered with apostrophes.

Propelled by sudden fear, I shouted out to them, lest, so intent on arguing, they drove off, forgetting they ever had a child.

They sat on the seawall by the car park, overlapping each other, edges smoothed over, and masks on tight. Through the eyeholes they pleaded with me, as if their lives depended on my collusion.

Then we went home.

HEATHER MCQUILLAN

This work was previously published in *Flash Frontier* (November 2015).

Trampolining in the Matutukiti

I reached the knoll first, nothing to boast of. My pack was lighter. Kyle carried both the Primus and the billy.

My hands were chafed from pulling myself skyward by tree roots. I raised them, let my heart's echo-beats subside. I inhaled the mountain's breath. *I am Hineahuone, a girl made from clay*. Kyle strode to the edge to take Rob Roy's photo. His lens focused on the mountain's white-crowned head, its chest – battle-scarred with waterfalls – its challenge.

Tarns, like torn patches of sky, littered the tussocks. On the next rise the bivvy sat, squat and orange. Beside it, the trampoline was a yawning rectangle.

I reached the hut first. As I lay on slices of glacial rock, heaviness ascended my legs, pressed my heart to the mountain. The taste of blood rinsed my throat. Cloud-swatches of greywacke painted the sky.

Jarred by grating pipes and screws as Kyle assembled the Primus, I rolled onto the trampoline's sun-warmed netting. My weight sank to unfathomable depths. I coiled to protect my bloated lungs. *Breathe out, clay girl. Breathe out.*

The billy simmered as I jumped – hesitant bounces at first, fearful that the *thwomp-slap-thwomp* would prompt an avalanche. Legs straight and bent, arms up and down. My body a curled ammonite, I bowed to Rob Roy in somersault after somersault. I sneezed.

While Kyle checked the map by Primus mantle, I counted the distances between us.

When daylight arrived, in cold slices of watermelon pink, the trampoline was gone. Kyle had already set off, not waiting for me to finish tying my bootlaces. The breath from my nostrils blended with the mountain's mist.

I reached the conclusion first but there was still the long walk home.

HEATHER MCQUILLAN

A version of this work was published in *Flash Frontier* (August 2016).

A mother's touch

The train pulls in to the sub-basement, where the dark masks the dirt and the faces of strangers. As they step onto the escalator, Ava feels it hum. Platform 3 awaits, floodlit with natural light that will expose every sweaty surface of the station, every muck-mouthed beggar sprawled among the coins that other people drop like waste.

Ava realises too late that her hand has brushed the rail.

'Don't touch that!' her mother snaps. 'Other people have touched it.'

Ava waits with her palms facing the sky and they shake in time with her sobs, while her mother springs a pump head of sanitiser from her handbag.

At home, Ava strips. Boils her clothes and her blankets, vacuums, swabs her bedroom with bleach-soaked paper towels, scrubs herself with steel wool and soap, and shuts her bedroom door.

'You're a good, sensible girl,' her mother hisses through the keyhole. Her pursed lips mist over as Ava seals the door with stretches of cling film.

'You'll be safe at least. I'll ride the train, I'll buy thin-sliced cheese.' Her mother's telephone voice pierces the layers between them.

Ava holds her palm out, scanning for any draught on which particles of other people might insinuate themselves. There are none.

Her mother leans closer, one palm flat against the door.

'I'll probably die of bacteria out here,' she ventures, and waits.

But Ava doesn't say anything, because all the words have already been used by somebody else. Instead, she stands in the middle of the room with her palms facing the sky. This time she doesn't cry. Her mother speaks again but Ava won't hear anything, because that's like holding something secondhand inside you. And Ava won't think anything, in case other people have already thought it.

Zoë Meager

A version of this work was published in *North & South* (11 January 2017).

Sharp stars

A woman and a child in a boat. Her child, and her other child, and her other. Her three children. And one life jacket.

She puts it on her youngest but her youngest slips through, and on the middle child, but the middle child slips through, so her eldest accepts it when the sea is calm and it clings to him while the sea boils and the youngest child is cut from his mother's arms, and the middle child is cut from his mother's arms by the raging world.

The sea spits out the hearts of ghosts. They drop like bombs into the bottom of the boat where they shudder and twitch until the woman collects them furtively, and her eldest child collects them secretly, and they hold the hearts to their chests until they are all beating to the same convulsive rhythm.

A woman arrives on shore. Her eldest child, vomit in his hair, drops a life jacket. Around them, wretchlings in tow of their mothers. Down on the sand, somebody weeps.

'Here are the codes to unlock your phone,' a stranger says. But the woman wants to know, where are the codes to unlock the world? There is a weak signal, and the voice of the man she loves comes through. 'Is that you?' he cries, and the line goes dead.

Roads stretch to the distance without north or south, but a woman and a child must set out. A paddock, an alleyway, a roadside camp. A woman and a child under a blanket, under a tin roof, in a tent. A woman and a child in a field, under a coat, looking up, seeing stars look down at them sharply, when all they have in this world are armfuls of hearts.

Zoë Meager

A version of this work was published in *To Carry Her Home* (Bath Flash Fiction, Volume One, 2016).

American Journal

Iowa House Hotel

In a dream last night we agreed on a course of action. *Here is our true north*, said the actors playing you and me. They shook hands.

One cooked for the other, one did the dishes; they measured their freedom by square metres.

In another dream, to a soundscape of elevator jazz, they found each other in a bar overseas.

You looked so much like you, so much as I remember.

The bartender said, *What'll it be?* You asked for wine, the person playing me asked for gin, typical.

Outside, because it was kind of London and kind of Jerusalem and sort of Chicago, the sky was a mash-up of glitter constellations.

Whoever you almost were in the dream – some voice inside a code of scents – tricked my mind.

You looked so much like you, so much as I remember.

Prairie Lights

Do you know where the poetry books are?
    Yes. No. Actually, just follow me.
    Here are the pages that survived the flood. Read them all quickly, before the waters rise again.
Like windows into a past we can't leave.
    Sort of.
And sunlight? Do you know where the sunlight is?
    Here, shimmering, in the bowls of my hips –

Nape?

    All sorts, really.

Should I read it in one go or take it a bite at a time?

    Why not, may as well. Read how you eat.

    Just follow me. I know the way, even the way home. The way to all the good stuff, every poem –

is aching for a place among the stars?

    Right.

COURTNEY SINA MEREDITH

This work was previously published as part of 'American Journal' in *Pantograph Punch* (February 2017).

A small holding

He shows me the first cage with all the pride of a parent. Inside, the black and white bird carols, its song both harsh and tuneful, then moves; clockwork-springing hops from perch to perch. 'Magpie,' he says, and rattles the side of the cage. 'Old Judas, here, he calls and another one comes.' He nods at the other cage and shows me how the trap works. 'Once it's in,' he twists his thick hands into a knot, 'I wring its neck. And then I bury it.' He misreads my silence, thinks I want more and smiles. 'The other day I caught one of 'em digging its way out. Had to fix the bugger twice.' He turns, gestures at the pleasance of paddocks, spreading out from under the macrocarpas. 'A small holding,' he says, 'but *mine own*.' Then he drapes his arm across my shoulder. It weighs me down, thrusting me feet first, into the waiting earth.

Vivienne Merrill

This work was previously published in *Flash Frontier* (September 2017), where it was dedicated to the memory of Sally Houtman.

In the playroom

The woodsman should not be trusted. Just because he looks gentle-eyed, his dove voice regularly charming; it does not mean he is what he says he is. The children tell their mother this but she does not believe them and shuts them in the playroom with their broken toys.

Hine is wise beyond her years according to the babysitter who often reads strange books to them. The last one frightened little Tane as it was about someone who didn't know what was happening to him. 'Kafka,' the babysitter said, 'was a genius.' The children do not care for geniuses – their mother always says *clever-clogs are socially isolated, lead lives of misery and usually die in servitude to some muse or other.*

The children don't tell the babysitter what they know. They have seen the way she peeps through the curtains when the woodsman visits and have heard her sigh.

Of all the toys, Tane wishes someone would mend his rocking horse, which he hasn't ridden since he was two years old. Hine is plotting a way to borrow the woodsman's tools from his vardo. *A little knowledge is a dangerous occupation*, her mother always warns, but Hine is well aware of the danger wood holds. The nasty splinters that result from badly-hewn horse's limbs can kill a child within twenty minutes. This fact will not hold her back as her birthday, in two days' time, will put her into double digits and render her invincible.

VIVIENNE MERRILL

A version of this work was published in *Flash Frontier* (May 2012).

Three minutes

The day we went to the fair you wore a yellow dress with red buttons shaped like hearts. You bought pink candyfloss and divided it into three. James ate his fast and you ate yours slow and I didn't really eat mine at all. James always sat next to you on the rides, so he could hold your hand. I sat by myself. When we got to the rollercoaster James said he didn't like the way it made his brain rattle in his head and went to buy hot chips. They said the ride would take three minutes.

As the car started moving and we climbed our knees touched and I put my hand next to yours I heard your breath catch in your throat when we got to the top of the track you wound your fingers through mine then we fell my stomach plunged my heart was beating so hard and you didn't scream not even when we went upside-down and when we stopped moving you smiled there was pink sugar glistening in the curve of your mouth I put my finger on your bottom lip and your tongue darted out to touch it so quick but you looked into my eyes the whole time in three minutes I made you mine.

When we got out James gave you a kiss and me the rest of his chips. At the bus stop you pressed something into my palm. It was one of your buttons.

Eileen Merriman

This work was previously published in *Flash Frontier* (September 2014).

Universe and Karl

It was a very nervous voice in the male choir. Karl's voice slid up and down as he stole glances at the boy standing next to him. Dark eyes, like espresso, that he wanted to fall into. Smooth, warm skin, like caramel. If he stood just a little closer, he could touch the delicate angle of Universe's jaw with his tongue. And then –

Universe Lau slid onto a top G, the glassy note filling Karl's chest. Karl, distracted, reached for a C and slid straight off the other side, crashing into a B flat. Universe winced. Karl fell silent, listening as Universe's notes soared into orbit.

Afterwards, the boys stood outside the school hall as they waited to be picked up.

Karl looked at their shadows falling in front of them and shifted, so they merged together. He said, 'Why did your parents call you Universe?'

Universe said, 'Are you tone deaf?'

A blue van pulled into the car park, four pairs of miniature arms waving out of the windows. It looked like a mutant beetle.

'Wow,' Karl said. 'Big family.'

Universe's mouth twitched. 'You should hear what they called my sisters,' he said, as he walked away.

'I like your name,' Karl called after him.

His words glanced off Universe's back. They fell into his shadow, now long and thin and singular.

The van door slammed shut. His Universe left. Karl lay on his back and waved his limbs around, a mutant beetle falling into a black hole.

Eileen Merriman

This work was previously published in *Flash Frontier* (June 2015).

Indian summer

It is the month of cicadas, a tamed sun, the air clear and forgiving. Somewhere a full tide laps on an underutilised beach.

The old father visits from his furnace in Australia. He is forced to stay at the last moment. No room at any other inn so he buries his hatchet temporarily and struggles up the stairs with his luggage to sleep on a mattress on the floor among the accumulated jumble of the spare room.

'You have so much shit,' he says to his son.

*

An old seaman in Sears khaki, he moves in pain and talks about how difficult it is living alone on the pension.

He has ritualised ablutions which last a minute and use the minimum of water allowing him to boast of a $30 water bill.

He laughs at her jokes, as an inescapable cost of accommodation. Accordingly she no longer has to agree with everything he says.

He tells her that suicides end up in some Indian level of hell being beaten on the feet with sticks by devils.

*

He takes a road trip, his son driving a hire car. It goes south with many misdirections to visit the urupa in a remote bay where his grandson lies. Apparently restless spirits have visited him since the murder. He wants rid.

He wants to go to the races but baulks at the $10 entrance fee. So he places a bet at the local TAB. His last trip he won $500 but this time he wins $15.

He says this is his last trip.

He says, 'I do not know if I will see you again.'

He takes his bag and walks out the open door.

Tofa.

He leaves behind a gutted packet of high dosage painkillers and a rebuking, troubling spirit.

Louise Miller

A version of this work was published in *Flash Frontier* (July 2015).

Instead of the madeleine

There is the young woman talking on the bus.

'Oh,' she says in summary of a reported confrontation, 'she was a real smart tart.'

I see my older cousin's bedroom with its drawn curtains, dim night-light and feel a rinsing wave of oppressive sorrow.

I see my older cousin. She is wiry-thin: petite is the word she dares to use. Catty is another word I use. My cousin watches her plate like an anxious bird, runs like the wind and is in all the A teams. Her appearance is a source of pride and so of shame.

She punishes herself with exacting housework. Her make-up is hidden deep in drawers away from her enraged mother. My own mother works for her sins so I am dispatched south, here into this fraught household during holidays. A fat pet to a cattery. My interests are reading, eating and proto-sexual. I am tolerated which weighs over the homesick days.

The silver lining within this prepubescent cloud is my cousin's copy of *Peyton Place*.

At night I move out of my single bed in that cold house and lie beside my cousin not touching. She holds the book and I read at an angle. I can read as quickly as my cousin runs. I skip over the redundant narrative to the hot tight places with their heavily freighted words. Trapped in my own excitement I wait long moments for her to catch up. My breathing slows and gathers weight.

Then her cold bony elbow jabs me. She claps the book shut.

'You think you are a real smart tart, don't you?'

I recoil in humiliation and yet simultaneously I see raspberry jam oozing out through golden pastry latticework, leaving a burnt skin on the black tray.

Louise Miller

The homecoming

After the tragedy, the wives of the crew became famous. Betty was the darling star; her husband was the captain of the capsule *Artemis* which had disappeared in space. She touched the nation's heart at the state funeral in her black Chanel dress, silk headscarf and dark glasses. Her face adorned *Time*, *Newsweek* and *Life*. Betty told the story of how her friends had been with her to watch *Artemis* approach The Anomaly and some network producer thought it would be great to have all her girlfriends on *Nightlight*. The show was a hit. Three months later the afternoon talk show *Space Wives* debuted. The girls talked with celebrity guests about the news, their lives and their passions. One emotional Monday afternoon, a panda-eyed Lana admitted to a struggle with the bottle and pills, Betty spoke about her abusive father, Laura launched her autobiography, and Peri spoke about her intense bond with her closest friend Inez. For three seasons their ratings soared.

And then Goldstone Observatory reported that signals from Major Alvin T. Moore's *Artemis* had returned to the capsule's point of disappearance. The heroes were finally coming home from the perilous realm of inverted space-time. The wives spoke first of relief, of closure, of how good it was that their husbands were still alive. They would deal later with the lost time. Then with just one day to go before splashdown Laura, Lana, Peri and Betty announced their homecoming special. They had something new and urgent that they wanted to say.

Harvey Molloy

Parting

They split the chattels in two. Half an eggplant sat in a half Tupperware container in what was left of the refrigerator. Half a television perched on half a cabinet. Half a Siamese spread itself over the semi-circle of the felted rug. My mother cut towelling lengthwise, sawed the dining table on a diagonal. It was a tough job, but she put the weight into her good arm. When she was halfway through she twisted an Oreo into fifty-fifty portions, and licked the film of icing from her biscuit. It was half good.

My father loaded up half a truck with chunks of art. The McCahon was guillotined so that my father was left with the 'AM', my mother took the 'I'. The kinetic sculpture was torched vertically and left two feeble arms that waggled in the wind. Pottery bowls were thrown at the concrete floor, and we measured out the fragments into Snaplock bags. The blue and green glazes shone like beetle wings. My father said he'd make mosaic frames. My mother said she'd make wind-chimes. I was half impressed.

Half a piano stood in my mother's study. She took the higher octaves. She sang the *Dr Zhivago* theme song in falsetto. The heirloom Bible was torn at the divide between the Old and New Testaments. We pulled pages from the classics and set them into two manila folders. Nobody wanted *War and Peace*, but my father took more than his share of the telephone directory and all the endings of Agatha Christie.

Later, my brother and I stood in the living room where bifurcated objects were being tossed into piles. *This is half-witted*, I would have said. But my half-tongue caught in my half-throat. My brother flicked me half of a smile, which looked sad.

Elizabeth Morton

This work was previously published in *SmokeLong Quarterly* (December 2015).

Stones

Do you know the way to a woman's heart is through the gallbladder? Tenderness calcifies in the exits, squats in doorways with hairspray and Cola.

A woman's heart is bile and fat. She swallows it back, sometimes. Sometimes she hoicks it into the sink.

A woman's heart is the kind of organ you keep in a viola case and leave on a train. Security will blow it. Smithereens.

It's casual terrorism – a woman explodes in an art gallery. A woman is on fire in the homeware store. A woman strips topless in Times Square and orchestrates her own rape.

It is an exercise in logistics. A woman can't read a user's manual or put together the flat-pack of where she is in the centre of things and down a bit.

Do you think a woman thinks of England? No. She's conjuring the Southwest, with canyons and cacti and jackrabbits that jostle on the dust road. She is the road.

A woman doesn't mind that you've run her down in your pickup truck. A woman blends in with the flora. A woman doesn't know what she wants, what she really really wants.

Sometimes, a woman's heart is mansplained by the court judge. Why didn't you use a clamp, the judge might say, but a woman just plays dead.

Years from now they will say Woman like it's allegorical. They will tell Little Goldenbook stories about the woman in sheep's clothing, the woman who cried wolf.

These days all the story books are empty. At bedtimes we collect gallstones in plastic cups.

All night, women pick at the glass ceiling like a scab.

Elizabeth Morton

The wheat field

On certain days in summer our wheat field becomes an ocean of rolling ochre. On days like these I am only eyes, ears, a nose, a mouth. I squint into midday sun until blue black crows morph into screeching sea birds and the Ferguson's barn creaks and groans like some long lost schooner.

On days like these the wind from the west wraps its way around lower legs and sinks feet softly into wet sand. On days like these I remember the road that wandered like us, hugged hillsides and promised eternity, where we stopped and ate grilled fish for breakfast and later found ourselves alone, on a stretch of white sand, watching triangle waves point and plunge, pound and pummel.

And I'm there.

From the back of the beach, light bounces off the chrome fenders of our Honda 50 as it rests against the solid trunk of an otherwise swaying palm and watches as our clothing comes off and piles into a heap, like the tangled limbs of lovers, next to a half-eaten mango that turns brown in the afternoon sun. We wade into warm water under a sky so infinite I almost cry. Your lips on my eyes, my mouth on your chest, my breasts are brown and our bodies meld together rocked by the rhythm of rolling waves.

'I put a baby in you.' Your proclamation is shouted back to the beach where I spread your T-shirt across the sand and let the earth embrace my bones, engulf my body. Where I doze and dream of the child that never is.

I watch and wait for you to surface, sometimes all day – until the sky is full of purple bruises, until the wind eventually dies, until this ochre ocean is just our wheat field again.

Linda Moser

A version of this work was published in *Flash Frontier* (August 2016).

Stoic

We couldn't cry about love because you just have to get on with it and of course there were the children.

We couldn't cry about desire unrequited because it's all a lot of water turned away from under the bridge, it might as well not be there, and of course there were the children.

We couldn't cry about a lot of things: the cancer and the soldiers and the repressive laws and the children, because of the supermarket, the surgeon, the car, the work, the appointments, the decimation of natural habitats, the finances and the decisions, the extracurricular activities for everyone, the aspirations, the deadlines and the dishes, which sounds silly but you know how it is. You have to get on with it.

We couldn't cry about the dishes, the driving, or the shopping still being there even with the cancer and the love and the lust and the children; because after all, you have to get it in perspective.

We couldn't cry about the house and the sale and the loss of profit because of the children and the chores and the cancer and voting the right way when everyone else voted the wrong way and protesting with placards, emails and Facebook petitions and of course above all again because of the children.

We couldn't cry about it because we weren't after all children and the children were crying about something else altogether, and they didn't understand, of course they didn't, they were only children.

We couldn't cry and there were reasons we couldn't cry and they became metaphors, vessels that both carried our tears and concealed them, because you can't, there's no point; the number of times we could have cried, you just wouldn't read about it.

Emma Neale

This work was previously published in *Sport 41* (VUP, 2013) and *Tender Machines* (OUP, 2015).

The changing rooms

Yes, a great change has come upon us. We attend the second-hand high school uniform sale. Cue cubicle shortage; cue queue. Cue acute kudos anxiety. Cue cuticles nibbled at for something to do. This scene is made of people desperately not wanting to make a scene:

Nervous kid mumbles, rolls eyes and tries to disappear into his shirt. Mother snaps at him, kid dies of embarrassment, mother has moment of regret, tries to soothe kid, kid dies again of embarrassment. Mother chooses clothes for kid, kid dies of embarrassment, kid is told to try on clothes, kid dies of embarrassment. Kid is shown where to get changed, kid dies of embarrassment; kid goes into wrong changing room, kid dies of embarrassment. Kid tries on clothes, they are the wrong size, kid has to come out of changing room to tell mother, kid dies of embarrassment. Kid has to try on another size, kid dies of embarrassment; another kid comes into the hallway, both kids die of embarrassment. Kid has the right size, has to tell mother, mother is talking to another mother, kid dies of embarrassment. Mother takes the uniform from kid, kid dies of embarrassment; mother talks to the school secretary while paying for second-hand uniform, kid dies of embarrassment. Mother asks kid to carry his own uniform, kid dies of embarrassment; kid goes to open the glass door out of the school reception and pulls instead of pushes, kid dies of embarrassment. Mother says, 'Are you okay?' Kid says, 'Yup.' Mother says, 'Is that all I get – *yup*?' But doesn't she know she's speaking to a dead guy? It's a miracle he can talk at all.

Emma Neale

It's cool in Katoomba

It's four hours since we arrived and I still haven't landed. It's cool in Katoomba and the sun shines around a mobile of cloud and kites of rainbows and the rain is another shape of feelings. We become tangled in knots of sheets like the unresolved talks in our minds, but a long bath from eucalypt-heated water and deep, warm sleep restores our balances. We work together making frames – it works, us working together – then we walk again in clouds beneath a sandstone bluff along the top of its talus slope, where waterfalls veil us in wet crystals, where eucalyptus bend and sway in silver-green cascades; and in the dry shelters where those angular masses have fallen from the faces the rock glows reddish orange. It's where cockatoos call in pips and squeaks and drop bubbles of song and the wood, it splits in splintering shatters of straight grain and cross, resonating metallic, those chunks of compressed lignins twisting, burning in the oven's slow heat, cooking porridge of mixed grains and rice. It's the pauses of sun and stratocumulus, the sedimentary strata, continental sandstones and haematite pans, those fine gravels that crunch underfoot above cliff walls in red heaths, blue heaths and black heaths with pinkish gold flowers, with your taste, with the wind of stars, the laugh you feel inside of me and the pause around which we revolve, in the dance of being, with more of us present when we talk of our families and their places in these events, the knot in the curtain opening two views of the garden, gradients of blues cooling to black and half-moons, temperatures hiding in the shade wet with ferns, and polynomials of shells, and jacarandas of parrots.

Piet Nieuwland

A version of this work was published in *Blue Five Notebook* (August 2013).

Five travellers in a small Ford

Five travellers in a small Ford travelled across the Ardennes. The Hautes Fagnes. The High Fens.

The fifth traveller, strapped in a car seat, cried with hunger.

Clumps of cotton grass rose from the bog land on either side.

The car pulled off the road for the fourth traveller to nurse the fifth traveller.

The sky was grey and despite the late spring there were patches of snow in the shadows.

The third traveller puzzled at his mobile as the navigation system was awry. Luckily, a signpost directed the travellers towards Eupen.

The second traveller, seated beside the third traveller, regretted not making muffins or packing fruit as, like the fifth traveller, the other travellers were hungry.

In 1940 Eupen was declared *judenfrei*. Its citizens celebrated.

The first traveller sat in the shadows of a deserted stadium and put his notebook to one side.

He was a liar.

There was no fifth traveller, no fourth traveller, no third traveller and no second traveller.

This was okay. For this is fiction.

In 1940 there were no Jews in Eupen.

This was not okay.

This was not fiction.

James Norcliffe

A version of this work was published in *Landmarks* (UK NFFD anthology, 2015).

Threshold

He was leaning up against the wall, his head tipped back to feel the cool of the paint when she arrived. He was clammy in his new shirt. He knew if he raised his arms now there would be dark sweat pools under his armpits. In the bathroom he'd looked at his pimply face in the mirror and willed himself a man, not a boy. He sensed the threshold under him, shifting beneath his feet.

He'd been there two hours already. *She said she'd come,* he told himself. The place was packed. People spilling onto the deck where the night air was biting, the smoke heavy and the cars raced past. The party was in full swing, all smoke and mirrors and crackle in the air when she arrived. He knew immediately when the quick tread of new footsteps entered the kitchen.

He couldn't stop himself stepping towards her voice, his heart jamming, despite the fact he'd only had the one beer. He gripped the now warm can. Rounding the corner he saw her in the middle of the kitchen, the low bare bulb behind her making a halo of her hair. She had her back to him, talking to another girl in their class; she was lifting the girl's new snake-like dreds in amazement, throwing back her head and laughing.

There was a perfect pause in the music.

'Rachel?' He almost didn't trust his voice.

She turned, seeming to take the whole of the light with her, that bare kitchen light and every other, holding for an instant all the light in the world in her hair, a blonde blaze as she spun towards him. 'Daniel!'

He thought he might go blind. 'Yeah, hey.'

She grinned.

He grinned.

And then she started to walk.

Heidi North

Evolving with energy drinks

skitterish under the weight of energy drinks, crazy man cometh, carnage in the kitchen, apologies, more cold cans in the fridge, chug 'em down, later in the day comes The Big Empty, all vacuous and throbbing, regrets and a soulless grin, sorry for everything I've ever done

can't sleep, can't stand being awake, sink another can cause it's not beer and it has vitamins, tell me mister that it's good for me, irritable at midnight out of answers, no more cans, walk to the service station, buy more cans, now it's more expensive than beer, drain another damn can

ring random numbers ask for myself tell them I'm a doctor, my hysterical laughter gives it away, on the flatmate's brake-less bicycle going to town, shoplift cans from supermarket, cop pulls me over – fined for no helmet, no light, too much chat but he drops me home, eat cold spaghetti swallow another can, count the paces around the house, pop pimples make instant coffee fill it full of sugar

sink the last can, out of money, lie down tortured begging God to shut my head up, start to believe in Jesus Christ, go to church kneel and pray steal from the donation bag, buy some more cans fall into a dribbling stupor lying on the couch watching a TV advert for Red Bull

Keith Nunes

Love poem

Houses are likened to shoeboxes, but shoeboxes are not likened to houses. A car is likened to a heap but a heap is not likened to a car. A child is a terror but a terror is not a child. A business might be a sinking ship but a sinking ship is no business. A bedroom is a dog's breakfast but a dog's breakfast is not a bedroom. A bad review might be a raspberry but a raspberry is not a bad review. A haircut is likened to a disaster but a disaster is not a haircut. Books can be turkeys but turkeys are never books. A holiday might be a riot but a riot is not a holiday. A garden might become a headache but a headache is not a garden. I dream about you but you are not a dream.

GREGORY O'BRIEN

This work was previously published in *Beauties of the Octagonal Pool* (AUP, 2012).

Closer and closer

She is a parachutist and for her own reasons approaches her family reunion from above. Falling, she spies a young girl who looks cool, dressed in fluorescent pink bike shorts, hair tied up with a scrunchie, which is a sort of mini deflated parachute for the head. It's a sign, the parachutist thinks, that I'm landing in the middle of the right reunion. Also she can see a group near a smoky BBQ, waving. The parachutist can't yet confirm that she's landing in the midst of the right people but she likes the look of them, the way they're starting to part a little so that she can land safely amongst them. Please, let them be my family, she thinks, because whoever they are, they're getting closer and closer.

RACHEL O'NEILL

This work was previously published in *One Human in Height* (Hue & Cry Press, 2013).

The children have grown

One day you look around and find that there are children who have grown monstrously large. They run but are lopsided. They grow silent in ways that seem to influence time. You are unsure that it is the right thing to do but you sniff socks, and open lunchboxes. The clues are scant, until you discover chat rooms that offer advice – the child is a magnet seeking its *little earth*, the lodestone that will secure its weight to the world. In the next phase the child will put on a mask. You are prepared. You know now not to use the little sewing scissors on the elastic at the back. The child must be the first to indicate whether they are staying in or coming out. You feel more confident and start to relax, until it hits you – where did these children come from? Who had them before you?

Rachel O'Neill

This work was previously published in *One Human in Height* (Hue & Cry Press, 2013).

Pretend I'm your mother

When I squeezed into the carriage on the Trans-Siberian express for a ten-day journey and realised there was nowhere to put my one small bag because I'd come in last and the five others had taken up all the space in the luggage racks and expanded themselves even further to fill the lower bunks plus hung stuff on the narrow ladder, when I realised I'd have to climb to the top bunk which was high up and which meant I'd have difficulty in the night negotiating my way to the toilet, which was way at the end of the train and always had a queue, I said to the youngest and least threatening-looking man in execrable Russian, *Pretend I'm your mother and move to a top bunk, please* – while lifting his legs and sitting firmly on the bunk, bag on my lap and smiling expectantly until he moved out – and he, groaning and muttering something that sounded remarkably like *motherfucker*, climbed the ladder to his new bunk, ignoring my *spasibos* until they became an offer of blinis and cheese and vodka.

Maris O'Rourke

Three firsts

One

He takes the baby out. Alone on the back seat for the first time his son begins to cry. Thrusts his legs out straight and throws his arms wide – like a panic-stricken starfish. A scarlet flush rises with his screams. White knuckles lock onto the steering wheel. It seems farther than one kilometre. He would kill for a cigarette. It's been six weeks since he quit. Finally he stops the car, kneels, leans into the anxious silence as their eyes meet.

Two

He arrives with the baby. Alone in the garden she is planning the first section of a walk – Te Araroa: The Long Trail – 3,000 kilometres from Cape Reinga to Bluff. She kneels, gathers up her grandson, folds him in a familiar fit. She sways and sings to him – just as she had with his father. His eyes sink to slits that widen in warning if she stops, or shifts, their shared rhythm. Finally, with a long sigh, he flops like a boneless jellyfish. Sleeps.

Three

He takes the baby out. Alone, for the first time since their son's birth six weeks before, she stands in the silence. Meanders to the garden. Meditates on the basil. Kneels into it. Inhales it. Crushes it. Chews it. Gathers it all. The sun slants onto the bench as she mixes the pesto's ingredients: fresh basil leaves, grated Romano cheese, extra-virgin olive oil, pine-nuts, garlic cloves and seasoning. As her milk comes in smells rise with her anxiety.

Maris O'Rourke

A version of this work was published in *New Dialogues and New Beginnings – Poetry Anthology 2013* (Printable Reality, 2013).

The dark

It's black, pitch black when I open my eyes, so I close them again. What's the point of eyes if you can't see anything? But I hear everything.

Mum loves Barry White. I've heard him so many times that I know all his songs off by heart. 'You see the trouble with me …' I must be real trouble 'cos she never lets me dance with her. When Dad comes home, they dance and sing. If I sing too, they laugh and laugh and start caterwauling.

Last week we went to the park. Everybody said I looked beautiful, my blonde hair a halo. I could be an angel. Mum laughed. 'Inside every angel, there's a little devil,' she said.

'Mum. She's doing it again, Mum,' he yells, standing in the doorframe, and my tell-tale brother gives me a smug grin. I give him a two-fingered salute.

'Just you wait,' he hisses. And I wait – one, two, three, four. Right on cue.

'Eve? Eve, how many times do I have to tell you?' The thud of her wooden clogs on the stairs beat out the familiar rhythm of her mantra.

How many times? Stupid question. *It's just the devil in me showing itself*, I want to say, but I know better.

It's still dark, Barry White is crooning and I can hear them moving about downstairs. I relight my candle and sit on the windowsill. Careful not to drop it like my devil wants to, I stare at the small dot on the horizon. It will rise slowly and we will walk to the park. By the time we return, it will be dark.

Eileen Palmer

Last ride

He woke at daybreak, went out, saddled his horse and rode away, leaving his parents asleep. He rode with a loose rein for he and the mare knew and trusted each other. Along the track by the creek, waking birds twittered in the ti tree and two ducks slid into hiding among the rushes. Obligingly he looked the other way.

Leaving the track, they climbed up through the pine plantation. He'd helped plant these trees. 'One day,' his old man had said, 'these'll build you a house.'

He, being a boy, had grinned and asked, 'How about a hut?'

Above the trees he reined in and looked out over empty paddocks. The stock had all gone last week. He lit the cigarette he'd filched from his mother's pack and asked himself what he was feeling. The answer was, mostly, nothing. He was over raging at his father's stupidity, the bank's shortsightedness. Now, he wanted to take all this: the pink tinted sky, the creek, the birds, the mingled smell of horse and tobacco; to package them up and keep them with him for ever and ever.

He would have stayed longer but he felt the horse growing restless. He wheeled her with his knees and they took the long way back. At the last paddock, he leaned forward and spoke. Knowingly, she flicked her ears. He nudged her with his heels, she broke into a gallop and he let the wind pull his lips back into a grin.

At the house, he slid to the ground, unsaddled her then laid his forehead against the smooth, warm neck for he loved her as he'd loved no woman thus far. He wondered where they would be in a month's time. One thing for sure. They would not be together.

Janet Pates

A version of this work was published in *Flash Frontier* (July 2012).

Not another story about love

I find myself writing yet another poem for you, and I wonder why I waste the paper. Surely a tree didn't give up its life just to be engraved with still more words about you. All those trees that have died for you over the years! Enough to provide shade for all of Auckland. I could have dedicated a park to you, rather than writing all that bad poetry. Yes, a park would suit you. Something a little overgrown, with paths that lead nowhere and have unexpected corners. And marshes with swathes of long grass to get lost in. And mosquitoes. Oh dear. If you were a park, I don't think sensible people would go there much.

Kiri Piahana-Wong

This work was previously published as one of 'Three' in *The Lumière Reader* (2008).

Quarters to spare

On the run, we spend a cloudless winter afternoon at a mom-and-pop motel after visiting the real Billy The Kid Museum. *He died as he had lived* you quote his tombstone and I call us boy bandit kings. We switch on the TV then jump on the bed that renders vibration: fifteen minutes for twenty-five cents. We have nothing smaller than the stacks of hundreds in the backpacks we carry. So, I fake-ID a bottle of Southern Comfort and saunter out with pockets jangling like spurs.

In our oasis, we strip to our superhero boxers and you anticipate the trembling as I feed the machine. Nothing happens even when I get irritated and hit it repeatedly with the butt of your grandad's antique Colt. Your homemade bandage weeps as you pull me down and we shake the bed ourselves. Midway through, CNN broadcasts our high school photos. I always hated that blank-faced picture of mine. We sneak out without returning the key.

Mesas and midnight surround us. The dashboard lights tell me I'm pushing beyond the limit. My heart lodges in my throat. I wanted so bad to protect you. All the money in the back seat means nothing, you'd say. Even though I once thought it could be everything. You lie with your face towards me, blue-tinged but still so beautiful. The desert is trickster country. Our outlaw love, a mirage of desperation. Those magic finger moments linger like moon-shadows as long as we have quarters to spare.

PATRICK PINK

Taking my boyfriend to his tangihanga

River mist dulls a morning sun like uncarved bone.
Green hills are cloaked in feathered winter white.
Abandoned outbuildings are ghost places with watercolour-smudged edges.
Power lines drape from pole to pole like a boy's scalloped attempt at ocean waves.
A lone hawk tags the blue wall sky.
Roosters strut a roadside picnic area like hungry restless warriors.
Frost lingers in a barn's square shadow.
Silos point heavenward like tarnished accusations.
The coffin lid is smooth though my fingers trace the wandering wood grain.
Jase's mum says she thinks his gumboots will fit me fine.

PATRICK PINK

This work was previously published in *Flash Frontier* (December 2016).

128 Abel Smith Street

the high wind has stirred thousands of dust particles that have become a mist hanging over the city in the early morning light that is a fragile pale blue similar to that of transparent bone china teacups/ the police have raided 128 looking for terrorist firearms and balaclavas/ 128 opposed the notorious traffic bypass/ they fix bicycles and grow vegetables and rent out their front room for community and political functions/ i was invited there once to read poetry and to listen to a musical concert/ like the old days of the *salon*/ and my friend Jackie Williams told me she was born in 128 when it was a nursing home many years ago/ and now Jackie has gone to the big *salon* in the sky/ the dust particles refuse to settle all morning they dance above the harbour making it look as if there are fires out at sea/ the police raid is in the news and has even reached the newspapers in Bangkok in London and in Istanbul/ a city council street cleaner wearing a fluoro orange waistcoat tidies up debris that came down onto Abel Smith Street in the high wind/ probably a security intelligence officer

Vivienne Plumb

A version of this work was published in *The Cheese and Onion Sandwich and Other New Zealand Icons* (Seraph Press, 2011).

Rites

As they wander to the site across the peat bed, they chat.
'Sacrifice.'
'Religion.'
'The acid should have preserved …'

Sandy particles had washed into dimples on the fresh washed surface. Some collected in curved rectangular shapes, interspersed with little dips. A string of dimples here, a circle there. The trodden footpath of the archaeologists' steps before they put down duckboards showed like a sparkling carpet.
'It's amazing how the peat saves everything.'
'But no bodies.'
'Not yet.'

On arrival at the dig, they watch students slice the peat away precisely and place it for the washers to process, dissolving each sod in water, filtering carefully for fragments in sieves.
'Nothing.'
'Just the shoes?'
'Yes. Perfect, aren't they?'
'We were lucky to find them. It's a miracle, you know.'

When she left, the sky was clear. Now, the wind was up, and the sky was greying. The rivulet was glistening in the sunlight that leaked under the growing clouds.

She always paddled in the water, for luck. Just a silly superstition, but every time she passed, she did it. So she took off her shoes and paddled across to the sphagnum on the other side. The storm suddenly broke as she wandered towards the trees, so she dashed into the copse for cover just in time, as hail cascaded down, followed by torrential rain.

When she got back to the brook it had broken its banks. She waited for it to subside, and then crossed to retrieve her shoes. They had gone. She guessed that they had washed downstream, but even after a long search, she realised that she had lost them. So she blessed the finder and returned, skipping in circles in the wet soil, delighting in her footprints, long and elegant, with five little dimples left by her toes.

Martin Porter

The New Zealand weather pattern

One minute, there we were, outside sipping gin and tonic in our sunhats (because we're sensible) and bikinis (all right, not *that* sensible), complaining about sunburn and water restrictions

washing day –
the first swallow
craps on my blouse

then *pow* – snow to seven hundred metres, and a windchill factor bigger than the prime minister's ego. Dramatic weather. I guess it's the price you pay for living on what is, after all, a pair of bijou semi-detached islands just north of Antarctica. It's like having an elderly neighbour who won't take no for an answer – *here you go love, a nice helping of polar airflow. No, no I insist. I was making a nice batch for myself and there's always heaps left over. What's the point, if neighbours aren't neighbourly?*

spring gale –
flowering against the hedge
　　　my red knickers

JOANNA PRESTON

Wintering over

Here, true winter comes stalking across the moor, bristling with Siberia. We retreat to the safety of our double-glazed burrows, spend winter severed from the world, gnawing through our stores of fat and familial tolerance. Waiting out the winter, until the nights too begin to shrink, and the sun makes a wobbly reappearance over slate roofs. Then we'll emerge, blinking in light become unfamiliar – every winter is the first winter, every spring is the first spring. Survey our neighbours; reckon the survivors.

unbroken snow –
the shadow of a stone wall
lengthening

Joanna Preston

A version of this work was published in *Yellow Moon* (December 2003).

Jack™

Let me introduce you to Jack. Jack is skinny and not especially handsome, but he's one of the hottest models working today.

Jack is our hero – he takes the flak before anyone else, saving us wear and tear. Here is Jack as battlefield medic, bending over a wounded soldier in combat fatigues.

Jack looks like a talk-show host. He has realistic degrees of freedom and joint limits. He has fully articulated hands and three pre-programmed grips. If for now his reach exceeds his grasp, well, it won't be for long.

Jack is equally at home on a tractor or in a submarine. He works in real-time inverse kinematics to help you design your world. He's worked for NASA and John Deere, conforms to US military standards and can perform full-scene anti-aliasing and record 60 fields per second. He is the proud sum of years of time and motion study.

But Jack is no dataset dummy. He's learning to listen. And soon, we will teach him to talk.

We are eager to hear what he will say. Jack, old buddy, what's happening? What's the gossip out there in dataworld – the whisper on the wires? 'Our reporter in the parallel universe, just-call-me-Jack, is online with a special feature …'

Jack is here to save us from ourselves.

CHRIS PRICE

This work was previously published in *Husk* (AUP, 2002).

The present

We four children were crammed into the back seat of the Austin Seven. My mother sat in the front. A hat perched on her head, lips pursed. It was Christmas Eve and also her birthday. My father drove silently to Gamages, a large department store. He parked the car and left without a word. Then the door opened and he got back behind the steering wheel. He dropped a parcel in mother's lap. It was a present. 'Can I open it?' She peeled off the wrapping paper to reveal a black handbag – unfashionable but serviceable. 'It was all I could afford,' whispered my father. 'It will do for shopping, I suppose,' said mother. It was handed to me, and we admired the shiny brass catch and the studs on the side.

winter twilight
a spark of light
from Big Ben

Dad drove on to Trafalgar Square so we could see the huge Christmas tree, donated to the British by Sweden. The post-war lights were bright and we got out of the car and bought a couple of bags of crumbs to feed the pigeons and some roasted chestnuts from a street vendor for ourselves.

in her cupped hand
the paper bag
rustles

Nothing could have been more splendid than to see the coloured lights after the blackouts of war. Mum and Dad were silent. The present lay forgotten on the back seat.

PATRICIA PRIME

This work was previously published in *Journeys: An Anthology of International Haibun*, 2nd edn (CreateSpace Independent Publishing Platform, 2014).

First fox

I went to London, once. I'd never seen snow before and on the first night it came spinning through the light of the streetlamps.

I'd fallen for a guy who ran a bar in Brighton. We'd gone to stay with his mum. The house was hot and had a potpourri stink. There was wine after wine. I tried to sit politely, but kept dashing to the window to watch snow thickening on the bushes outside.

I didn't know where to put my elbows at dinner. I knocked over my glass and Pinot Noir bounced off the table, splashing his mum's pale silk blouse. Oh, don't worry, my dear, she said, dabbing it with her napkin. Drunk as I was, when she looked at me then I felt the same oily shiver as when I'd glimpsed eels sliding across paddocks back home.

I wasn't allowed to sleep in Connor's room so he snuck down three flights of stairs to mine. I woke with him lying on top of me. Snow glinted past the window above his head. Then he crept back to his room.

In the morning, I opened the front door. The air was sharp as Champagne. The sun cleared the clouds and the white garden burst into crystals.

I rushed out and made snow angels. I threw snowballs at a tree and stood beneath screaming when ice lumps broke on my head. The snow tasted delicious, metallic and pure, and crunchier than a slushie.

'Bounds about like a dog,' I overheard his mum grumble as I went back up the steps.

'You're letting out the heat,' she said.

I turned to close the door and saw a red shape blaze across the snow.

We caught the next train back to Brighton.

He never called again.

Leanne Radojkovich

A version of this work was published in *Flash Frontier* (July 2015) and *First fox* (The Emma Press, 2017).

Changing course

I worry we'll be lost in the forest of crying pines. I want to find the sea, to reach the beach. You say, 'Trust me,' but I don't, we argue, sand in my throat. I want to claim the dunes, the bathing shed, the outside shower. I know exactly where Aunty parked her car under this tree, over here where Uncle swam nude at night alone, where the men from Taiwan caught the crabs, where we built a fire with your father, cooked *snarlers*, drank wine, where my dad knelt in trousers to drink tea … how he hated sand and how silly I looked in my cut-away togs with my waxed, bruised thighs.

We're going forward. I can no longer claim to have lain on that bank in my bikini and they've moved the herons too so we can cycle through to Richmond close to the road where we waited by the mouth of the sea on school mornings with our net and a milk bottle for the whitebait. Where's the scout hall, the footbridge, the rubbish dump, the catch-in-the-back-of-my-throat, freshly-killed-meat smell?

All my secret roads are gone and our river's changed course.

MAGGIE RAINEY-SMITH

A version of this work was published in *Flash Frontier* (October 2013).

Boil up

'Smells good; you cookin' up another one of those bloody poems of yours, mate?'
offered my gap-toothed neighbour, through the interrupted picket fence.

'Reckon,' I said, *stirring* up a bit of everything on the page.

'Hope it hasn't got all of that silly fancy shit; those clever-dick tricks & *run arounds*?
Gotta give us plenty of good old carrot & onion words, yunno!'

'I'll try,' I lied, chucking in a couple of audio-dacious *slap, cackle & plops*
& one or two cacophonous condiments, when he wasn't looking.

I makamaka ana ahau ko rua ngā kupu Māori hoki, nē rā –
just to make the broth more existentially authentic.

By now the pot lid was arguing back at me, quite brazenly *springing* up & down,
telling me it was having trouble keeping all the stuff inside in line & that nothing
was rhyming up anyway.

'Remember, mate, don't overcook this one, eh! Last one you served up
was too bloody lumpy & tasteless. Give us a real boil up this time,'
so sniffed my whānaunga, picking his nose behind a palisade.

'Yeah, yeah,' I muttered, alternately alliterating
& assonancing the concoction with a wooden spoon.

But – toward the end of our mōteatea – I did turn down the heat a bit
& dressed up a little watercress on the side.

Reckon there's no need for any more of this half-baked verse stuff around here, eh.

mā te wā.

VAUGHAN RAPATAHANA

Author's note

i makamaka ana ahau ko rua ngā kupu Māori hoki, nē rā: I threw in a couple of Māori words also, eh.

whānaunga: blood relative.

mōteatea: song-poetry.

mā te wā: see you later.

A version of this work was published in *Plate in the Mirror 2016 – Poetry Anthology* (Printable Reality, 2016).

Folly House

5:45pm. Guy knocks. He has something very important to say. He is now 'a ball of pure consciousness', and we must all 'derelativise' ourselves to become 'pure consciousness'. He has de-Freudenised himself and understands all his blocks and complexes. He no longer feels any sexual desire. He has also de-Marxised himself and burns a pound note by way of demonstration. He has recognised many 'happy coincidences and omens', such as his twenty-first birthday falling on Ascension Day. Outside it's getting dark, spring-chilly, the grey river moves under Folly Bridge and past Folly House where Guy walks about, chainsmoking Gauloises, completely assured, hands shaking. He has realised that he has 'impeccable taste' and that Gauloises are the only cigarettes, Bach the only composer, Conran's the only dinner sets. He has a reading list of the Books: Shakespeare, Keats, Isherwood. Everything has led to this moment in time and to him being who he is. When the dons read his philosophy papers in Finals, they will at once see the truth, and the good news will break very soon afterwards.

Harry Ricketts

A version of this work was published in *Half Dark* (VUP, 2015).

The storm

Monday, July 3rd: Rain and flooding in Auckland – an anticyclone over the South Island keeps the weather stalled in the North. Coromandel takes the brunt. The creek's up. Your shoes are sodden, socks soaked through, raincoat ineffective. But you've done your walk.

The Perfect Storm 'hits' today – so do school holidays: the gang's all here, clustered round the cardboard display for *The Road to El Dorado* – 'It's really funny when *these* three guys call *those* two gods,' explains a small(ish) boy.

Girl with steel comb
like fangs
adjusts her hair

Cheekfuls of popcorn
keep the boys' mouths shut

Everybody's got a radio, everybody's mouth is open, screaming out instructions, commentary … It's quite a storm.

Dem waves iz beeg
I hope we don't git sunk
Git outta *dere!*

Jack Ross

This work was previously published in *Haibun Today* (1 May 2008).

One aisle over

Driving from Yosemite he says he's busting and he can't hold on for the life
of God and Jesus to boot

before the car is even parked he's racing to the Mohave market with the single moms
outside next to the carts with the tag *do not steal, property of*
that you see outside every market in America
peeled baby carrots, hummus and a trashy magazine
are gathered in the interim before he reemerges slowly
spent like a dam now dry and a goofy grin, apologetic from all the urgency
the short woman at the check-out stand is waiting and
starts yip yipping like a chihuahua

friendly until she sees his T-shirt with the men pushing red wheelbarrows over the proclamation,

– we don't need the boss, the boss needs us!
yap yap!

– excuse me? we didn't hear you, we say.

– swamp thing! she tells him. You better go back to Santa Barbara.

Everyone is a stranger someplace.

Nina Seja

A version of this work was published in *trout 12* (2004).

Sinfonia

My fingers roll upwards and I am in a cathedral. The orchestra may be small but it fills the church with smug sobriety. The little French notes that chip away at the chords are blasphemous. They are imps, teasing the brown-skirted monks processing up the aisle. 'Dance with us,' they giggle. 'There will be no dancing in this church,' intone the outraged Germans. The march finishes and I am alone.

'*Stille Nacht*, but not so *still*,' says Sebastian. The left hand has become a ceaseless foot-fall. The right-hand air is written on the page like a single embroidered thread, led by a needle that cannot see where it is going. I know this by heart but must read the pattern anyway because I am only a servant. A voice sings of loneliness, without a breath.

But there is still trust. A column of sunlight emerges through a crack. The stitches unravel gloriously where I have stopped trudging.

Ha! A gypsy stomps into view. She poses, proudly tapping her bare foot and bullies my heart-ache away. 'This is no time to mope!' 'Agreed,' says another and the two of them weave a sweaty duet, prodding me to join them. I forget the monks and strut too. Even though it is the key of grand drama, my heart lightens and I know there are more dances to come.

I am a heathen but when I play Bach, I believe in God.

Kay Shacklock

A version of this work was published in *Flash Frontier* (February 2016).

The deer builds a portaloo

The deer valued his environment and enjoyed privacy, so decided to build a portaloo. He sent for instructions from his daily newspaper, *Cervine Today.* A Black Forest manual written by conservationist Herr Kessler arrived. How simple he made it seem.

The deer couldn't read German but was always one for innovation. He pulled armfuls of fern to create a cabinet. He took large river stones and lined a deep hole. He cut a manuka branch and fashioned a seat.

The question was whether to leave the lid up or down.

When he sat on the portaloo behind the great west wall of the forest listening to recordings of birdsong, it seemed ridiculous.

He decided to do what he'd always done.

KERRIN P. SHARPE

This work was previously published in *There's a Medical Name for This* (VUP, 2014).

For Pepper

Just the three of us these days. We hadn't seen Mandy for weeks, and Pepper was only a ghost now. So we went along the tracks, sound of our boots loud on the gravel.

'Problem is,' said Jay, 'is that we need chicks to take to the ball.'

Trix was up ahead. All in black, she clomped on, hating the school ball.

'If we can't get chicks,' Jay added, 'we should just go by ourselves.'

'There must be loads of chicks who just go with their mates.' I was thinking of Mandy. Last time I saw her she was wearing a petticoat and black lace-up boots, knees pink in the cold. Her eyes, rimmed in black, were searching the sky, like she could find Pepper up there.

'Course,' said Jay. 'Won't be the same – '

He meant last year's ball, when Jay and me and Pepper got drunk and fell about on the grass outside the gym.

'Those were the days,' I said, feeling about thirty.

Trix was climbing up onto the gravel shoulder. 'Train!' she shouted.

Me and Jay got off the tracks too. The snout of the train engine came into view. I saw myself flash in front of the train engine, my body flying over the trees. That was when Mandy appeared out of nowhere. She looked like a Valkyrie, hair loose down her back, then she raised her arm.

'This is for Pepper!' she screamed, and hurled a rock at the train.

My mouth fell open. The rock smacked into one of the windows, commuter faces mooning out at us. The window shivered with lines like a spiderweb. Then the train squealed and started to stop.

'Run!' shouted Jay.

No questions, we ran – towards Mandy, who was flying along the middle of the road.

TINA SHAW

Kalos

They taught you how to breathe. They shaped out your lungs and you practised inhalation and exhalation, over and over again, so much that they nicknamed you Aphrodite and lined your heart with gold. But you kept staring at the sun until your eyes burned and till all you saw was white light, like a poisonous heaven. So they scolded you, taped the night over your eyes, and you sat there motionless for hours, staring at a pool of metal not unlike the one in your lungs. Not unlike the tasteless sun.

They scattered your heart away later that night. Ripped half of it from your chest and turned it into dusty confetti till your pulse points felt like emptiness. You told them about stars and they scoffed, twisted your veins until they dulled into silence, and all the blood stuck together like glue.

'Stop looking,' they said. 'You're turning your heart into a stomach ache.' Like they knew how it felt to have near miss after near miss graze your skin, spill blood onto the cracks in the floor. So you sat there with a plane ticket in your pocket and when they decided it was time to teach you to sing, you ripped silver from the wallpaper and wrote down all the scattered pieces. Italy. France. Anywhere. And you stuck them onto your lungs for some day, one day, when you'd finally be brave enough to run away.

Emma Shi

A version of this work was published in *Flash Frontier* (April 2014).

The moon by train

1967. Kathie's twelfth winter. She travels overnight, six hundred and eighty-two kilometres nearer ice with her mother and Teenie, fourteen in dog years, ninety-eight had he been born human. With smiles and pats, they encourage him to sit beside a metal cage, above carriage wheels. Kathie worries. Isn't Teenie exposed? He manages a tiny wag of stump of tail but his irises are black moons afloat across their whites. Head drooping, he follows, sits on straw. The locomotive accelerates, whistle blows and Kathie remembers other friends, the ones she leaves behind.

The train rockets through darkness punctured with golden rectangles – suburban planets – where families watch TV, warmed by fires and mugs of steaming cocoa. Here, heaters aren't working, Kathie doesn't sleep – is unprepared for outer space.

Stopped. Eyes cupped, peering through glass – a sign, 'National Park,'– is pinned to mountains of pitch. She follows a point of light, bobbing closer, notices ash – no, snowflakes – seen for the first time, flitting on gusts of air, thinks of Teenie, black on black, this longest, coldest night of the year.

Morning. Her father meets them, rolls rotund Teenie out. He plumps to ground, stiff, lifts and drags his body along platforms of a new city. The house is sparse. They warm sausage and water, feed and wrap their doggie in hotties, moving blankets and Kathie's whole-child-body hug. They sleep.

Two winters, two houses later, Apollo 11 lands. Human beings first walk on the moon. A high-school first year, Kathie surfaces, at home, as usual, calling – but no arthritic wag, no bared teeth, no Teenie rendition of a human grin. Mum turns from dicing dinner, fixes Kathie's gaze with hers, nervous. 'The vet put him to sleep today.' Mum revealing only her sad back, says, 'If you'd known, he would've known.' Kathie remembers. Black irises. Bright moons.

Cherllisha Silva

Gone to sea

He lay very still, arms resting along his sides, and felt the gentle sway as the ocean caressed the hull. It was a calm night, the fishing good that day. Soon the journey home would unfurl before them, where they could collect their money and unwind a little. Warmth fluttered through his groin as he imagined the fiery heat of liquor and the company of a lady for the night. It had been a long time since he had seen land, prepared his own food, or taken a piss according to his own demands, and he was ready. Abrupt rhythm unnatural to the sea broke through his revelry. He opened his eyes and saw a woman dressed in blue, bent close as she fussed over lines and monitors, insistent electronic beeping filling the space between them. He said nothing, meeting her eye and looking deep inside, his breath now coming in shallow drafts. He was always restless when on land, the unyielding nature of earth and rock combined with the expectations of family somehow tying him down. He closed his eyes once more and returned to the lapping waves, creaking boards, the tang of fish guts mixed with engine oil – all that he called home. No one could hold him, the pull stronger than a mother's embrace. He was a fisherman, and the sea was where he belonged.

Rebecca Simons

A version of this work was published in *Flash Frontier* (October 2013).

Fisheye

The big one's head they have to hack off to fit it in the tub. But even then the bugger won't tuck, a fin stuck out the chilly bin, scales as chunky and sunlit as the packed out ice. They're grinning like bastards when they hump it up to the weigh in. 'Bloody good crack at First this year, boys.' They dig for it in the knock of ice, flop it down, silvery, with a crisp thud. The added head leaves good frills of blood on the tray. 'What y'reckon, eh?' 'Could be. Could take her out.' Its eye is a disc of tightened slime, yellow trim with a stud of black jelly. Specks of sky could go queasy and stretched in its lens – if you look too long. But they don't check out shit like eyes. They get into brews while the bloke makes a note of the kilos. The prizes, dumped on the pool table, will take more than a few cold ones to get to.

The back of their necks feel near third degree and the grass feels like it needs anchoring. Still, they'll last, as long as Kev doesn't start up again about his wife. Out on the water he'd tried it a couple of times but the chop was too stubborn and the catch too thick and fast to give him a proper shot. The poor bloke had zero clue – you wouldn't credit it. They cast out and yanked back trails of prime, while Kev tried to whine about intimacy. The fish shut him down all gasp and wing. The boys grinned into buckets at their tinfoil fits, their jaws adrift in throes of wet freckle. First is a trip for two to the Islands. Let's face it: any one of them could take Kev's wife.

TRACEY SLAUGHTER

Skyscraper, moon, sea

There's a skyscraper being made in the neighbourhood, maybe seven times higher than the buildings around us, and the rent will probably be that many times higher, too.

It is still wrapped in scaffolding nets, so we can see an absurd amount of artificial green by day, and in the evenings, when a strong light is thrown from the very top, there is always shadow, whatever the phase of the moon.

I once walked home across a moonlit mountain. The mountain was the centre of an island – one boat travelled to one side, another boat to the other – and I would cross the divide when the moon was in its fullness. I passed caves, one-room schools, scarecrows, chickens, two beaches, and when I opened the front door, sometimes I waited to turn on the light, wanting to stay in the mid-darkness a little longer.

A writer from a very quiet island once came to the city. One night, as we waited at a cross-walk, we looked up at a mass of green scaffolding and called the netted wall a vertical tropical sea. Another one of our pretty lies.

Madeleine Slavick

This work was previously published in *Fifty Stories Fifty Images* (MCCM Creations, 2012) and *broadsheet: new new zealand poetry 09* (May 2012).

Daffodils

Take it, she says. *You'll love it. Trust me.*
What is it?
A daffodil, she says.
I love her, so I trust it.

I trust this. This trust, this feeling of trust, I trust it, I think what I feel, I feel I know, and we're dancing; she's so beautiful, flowers in her hair; not daffodils, no, something else but they're beautiful and she smells so sweet, or is it the flowers? This free feeling, this feeling of freedom, this is what they're searching for, what they want in life; they want life, life without borders, without the edges that separate us from each other, and we're not separate now, we're together and it's beautiful, and she's laughing but it sounds like she's screaming, but maybe it's me and I think that she's crying, but I can't be sure because the lights are so bright I can barely see in the shadows; I can hardly see her through her tears, tears of anger, hate and she hates me and I don't understand as the blood spills from her mouth, is she bleeding? Her head snaps back and forth, and there's blood and I don't understand, and I try to hold her and I try to keep her safe but she won't talk to me, won't look at me, won't even move, and we're rocking in the lights; back and forth, back and forth as the lights flash, painting the walls blue and then red and then blue all over again. The stranger is in my face and he drags her away, he pushes me down, but I'm not paying attention; I'm looking at my hands, my bruised and swollen fists, bloodied and sad, and that simply can't be a broken tooth embedded in my knuckle; there must be some mistake.

D. F. Smale

Silence

On the first day pressure built. Her voice subdued, waded through air dense with accusations to reach him.

He sought answers in the yellowed pages of an anatomy book. The tympanic membrane, taut across his auditory canal. He poked around, a half-moon of bitter wax under one fingernail.

On the second day noise retreated further. It raised a white flag of surrender and disappeared behind a grassy knoll.

She stood too close. He watched her mouth open and shut, open and shut. Letters formed at her lips and bundled themselves into words. They bounced off his eardrum and spilled out to trickle down his cheek. No sound, only the sharp bite of her exhale.

By the third day he could feel the air vibrate as she walked towards him. Dry lips swept his cheek with a thousand tiny cells. He knew what would come next, how it would play out. The door would close behind her, its echo paired to the pulse of blood in his head. Then silence, solid and welcoming, would envelop.

Rachel Smith

The window is closed

The window is closed. A column of light between the curtains. Two stones wrapped in my left hand. Clench, unclench.

You will be sitting on that ugly floral bedspread, trying to find a foothold, a place to rest your eyes, where the room will again be your own. A diary is in the third drawer, the one that sticks as you slide it open; a book beside your bed. If you lie back, a constellation of discoloured paint where we scraped stickers from the ceiling. Their faint glow a world away from our bodies.

You are waiting, or not.

My fingers peel open, palm a map of indentations. Two stones with roughened edges of winter sky and concrete pillars. You would tiptoe tender across gravel to the river. Chill water took our breath – jump in, don't think, just in and under. In warm shallows, the current gently combed your hair downstream. Bare skin baked on sun-warmed stones. Your lips tasted of sweet river-weed.

You are waiting, or not.

The light moves – a curtain brushed or moon shadow tease. The window is closed. Gravel cuts now. Clench, unclench, scratches and scrapes. I throw, glass pings; my aim is always good. Clouds shift, light flickers. Breath from a ghost. Soft skin, sharp-edged words.

I take the last stone with me. Sit it on my windowsill until it is no longer mine.

The window is closed.

Rachel Smith

This work was previously published in *Flash Frontier* (August 2016).

Salt

1. Truisms: The sun rises; weather changes; no judge worth his own would find you guilty of slaying a guest who seasons their food before tasting it.

2. Pythagoras knew the triangulation between you and your parents: sun and sea. Derived from, but other.

3. Elizabeth I was insistent; only The Uncorker of Ocean Bottles could release the offerings from the brine.

4. Fish and chips are better by the sea. Taunting the tide with how far we've come.

5. So they went up to the Mock Turtle, who looked at them with large eyes full of tears, but said nothing. His ducts were merely secreting. Alligator tears.

6. She gifted me a cubic crystal from Grassmere's evaporation ponds. Halite, from the Greek *hals* or *halos*; hers slipped off between my lover's sheets. Cool – stripping the moisture from all it touches.

7. Tears are one third as salty as the sea. They drown as easily.

8. In the darkest depths, gypsum flowers.

9. Chinese snow, from bat guano, burns purple. With sulphur and carbon it makes fire medicine that can feather the sky, delight or slay those not on God's side. He sided with the alchemists.

10. In the Amazon, butterflies drink turtle tears. In Madagascar, moths with a proboscis like a harpoon suck on the tears of the sleeping magpie robin.

In Thailand, native bees sup on the tears in human eyes. Everywhere else humans draw on mermaids' tears for sustenance.

11. 'One in ten thousand reacts to the anaesthetic; one in twenty-five has permanent nerve damage. Shall we go in?' Scalpel through the neck to the saliva ducts, carving out the sialoliths therein. 'You're forming your own internal rocks,' he said. 'You, horses, and ninety-year-old men.'

12. *Sal sapit omnia.*

13. Unexpected on pineapple.

VIVIENNE R. SMITH

A version of this work was published as part of 'Salt/Pepper' in *takahē 82* (August 2014).

Pepper

1. At the back of the farm, up a hill, slippery in size-five gumboots: a blotchy red-leaved tree, a brother's wide-grinned bet, a mouth burning with insults.

2. For Hogmany, or any time she felt at year's end, she made Black Bun. Not a pinch, but grind upon grind on the mill's coarsest setting. A whisky for the pastry. A whisky for the filling. Another to line the tin and the stomach to last the drop.

3. He joined the force of good: car chases and sirens. She worried for him. Pepper-sprayed three times in his first year. So much for colleagues.

4. To evict ants: sprinkle cayenne or cinnamon. To deter snails: sprinkle cayenne, crushed eggshells, pine needles, thistle leaves, grit, gravel, human hair, grey lint from a clothes dryer, dust-bunnies from under the fridge, soft coiled belly-fur from roadkill cat, shadow-blue bellybutton lint from thirteen flaxen-haired virgins, star-drift fur from the rabbit in the moon.

5. The moon fell, as did I. Earthward amongst the kawakawa. Pepper is black and hath a good smack.

6. How far would the Queen go to flavour her meat? Why, to the ends of the world. 'Love will flow from trade,' she said, king-hearted to those battling monsters.

7. Dispenser holes too small for the cracked grains. Salt moist and clinging. Eggs naked and ashamed. I so miss your cruel breakfast headlines.

8. Capsicum traffic lights: red, orange, green. Green for go, so best avoided.

9. Mammals feel the burn of capsaicin. Not birds. Birds could be peppered all day and not feel it internally, unless the buckshot hit muscle or blood.

10. Every family is dysfunctional, including the nightshades: potatoes, tomatoes, eggplant, capsicums, Cape gooseberries. Bitter, gut-wrenching disputes over drug consumption.

11. Surprising on strawberries.

VIVIENNE R. SMITH

A version of this work was published as part of 'Salt/Pepper' in *takahē 82* (August 2014).

Engageantes = detachable sleeves

Elizabethan sleeves could lie flat in a trunk like fish. They could be carried on two straight extended arms. Curved where they joined the shoulder, tapered at the wrist. Tacked in, when required, by skilful hands.

'Which sleeves on the morrow, My Lady? Which jewels?'

For the sleeves had jewels in plenty, embroidered birds, fawning flowers, hunting hawks, stags and deer. A whole landscape, one's whole social position on a sleeve.

Oh, quick with the sleeves, seamstresses.

One on either side, each carrying a fish. Racing to get it in. The ruff for the neck, the bodice that narrowed the waist like the neck of a lute.

Stand up, My Lady. The sleeves are in.

Walk with a gliding step.

Look serene. Your sleeves will save you. Your sleeves are angel wings.

NB. They are not worn on the scaffold.
They will not fall on the straw.
But you will be carried out like a sleeve to St. Peter ad Vincula.

ELIZABETH SMITHER

Spider-Man blue

Rosie notices first. 'Where's William?'

Gareth stands up, feeling yesterday's game in his knees, his hips. A beautiful day, the first good one of summer. The park is full of running kids but no sign of Will. He's always been an explorer.

Gareth walks down by the weeping willows, down to the river. A huge boulder stretches out over the water. He's seen older kids up there before. Good spot for sunbathing, or a sneaky cigarette.

A flash of red and blue up there. Gareth lets out the breath he didn't know he'd been holding. 'There you are,' he says, forcing a smile into his voice. 'Get down from there, buddy.'

A six foot climb. No idea how Will managed it. Gareth struggles for footholds, jandals slipping across the stone. And no idea, once he's up, how he's going to get them back down again.

Will wears a Spider-Man suit, a cousin's hand-me-down that he loves even though it doesn't fit. He's always tripping over the legs. He's standing at the edge of the rock, where the older kids jump. Twelve feet to the water, but not a straight drop. You've got to go out a fair way to make it to the river. The older kids take a run at it.

Gareth moves slowly. 'Come on, mate,' he says. 'Let the river be.' He pulls Will into an embrace. 'Got you. You had me worried. Let's go back to Mum.'

Some nights he dreams in Spider-Man red and blue. He'd burn the world to bring those colours back. But in the morning the truth is green and yellow. The sides of the ambulance, reflected in the thirsty brown water.

Grant Stone

Thomas

He's a bit old for throwing tantrums. He smashed carved crucifix, hurled guaranteed jewels and hiffed books out lacy windows. Flattened her azaleas on the other side. Mary looks down and sees an old man curled on the floor. Spent, he flickers back to the days before he met his love.

The only news all weekend was he was up all night singing songs.

They moved him to another room so the others could get some sleep. Left him to it, to become a baby bird. Tiny purple tongue sucks drops, not ready to fly just yet. My mother wants me to smother her with a pillow if she ever gets like that.

Tomorrow I drive to pick up replica vertebrae from a whale and kiss this dying man. After lunch I'll lurch up around the twisty driveway over humps through automatic doors onto vast swathes of floor. Yellow and pink blooms scattered on black mass. This bed of bones has a heart as strong as an ox.

M. B. Stoneman

On Godley Head

We park the car at the end of the road. The day has not yet decided to clear; it is perfectly windless, and mist throws a milky veil over the scarred hills, tinged with early summer green. We take the right-hand path along the top and walk silently together, passing under some huge battered pines. Far below the Pacific is a blank slate for our thoughts. The strip of beaten earth between the thick grasses grows narrower; we walk in single file. The path peters out and I sense we are close to the edge of the cliff. We come to an awkward halt – you on the path while I take a stance above. There are hundreds of birds, gulls, cormorants, terns, looping and diving in the sky ahead of us. I watch their manoeuvres, see a tern swerve to avoid a gull. Their cries are a vast cacophony expressing all the emotion we cannot. Now you do say something. I see your lips moving, but my ears will not hear.

sun over the sea
a tiny yacht sails
outside the heads

Barbara Strang

A version of this work was published in *Kokako 10* (April 2009) and *Crest to Crest* (Wiley Press, 2009).

Eye contact

M is for magnetic

M is for magnetic. Have you noticed the finite time strangers make eye contact? One-point-one milliseconds.

I tested it once. I stretched it to three seconds. He didn't look away. He was a crumpled blond with surf-blue eyes, untangling from a Western-bound window-seat sleep. I sat alone across the emptying carriage. He wasn't supposed to keep looking.

The electric train hummed, gutless. Too quiet. The white walls glared. He made me feel like a poster-board screwed high in Aotea Square, two-dimensional behind glass. I hunched into my sleeves and watched for Sunnyvale.

I would rather be loved for my soul.

O is for open

O is for open. A pair of Pasifika boys, black-haired and walnut-skinned, laughed and jostled each other, chasing the rubbish truck down Sunnyside Road. It had just rained, and there was an unearthly glow to the trees, less scrape and more swish to the pavement. The scent of wet earth lingered. The long-haired one spied me and yelled, 'Hello!' with a grin. They scrabbled to clear a spilled box. His enthusiasm surprised me. He shifted his construction orange coat and lifted a box with lean arms. I could hear him singing, 'Soleeeee,' as the truck flew them round the bend.

KIRSTEN STROM

Parade

The cars were big-as 'n slick like Obama would use, eh. We were piled in, cuffed in case we got any funny ideas. The prison was munted so they had to get us out, relocate us up north until they fixed up all the quake damage. The cars were meant for all the dignitaries 'n such and the cops that were down for some drill exercise for the Rugby World Cup in case some shit went down with Al Qaeda. But after the quake and what-not the cars were used to shift us around. Those cars were smooth man, I haven't felt prouder getting into a vehicle since the day I bought my Ford and she was a beast, man. Up and down the streets I went in her, hole in the exhaust, belting with the sounds of the engine and AC/DC… thun-der, nahnahnahnahnahnahnahnahnah thun-der. Man, I was important behind those cylinders.

Anyway, we rolled down the streets in the flash motors. It was early, eh, but there were these kids out on the road in their PJs and they started waving at all the cars cruising, only doing twenty. Those kids waved at us – hard out man. One kid was jumping up and down. I felt important – like some swanky Santa or something. I waved back, even though I was cuffed and the glass was tinted so they couldn't see me. I said to the driver, 'C'mon man, do a wheelie for the kids,' but he kept staring straight ahead, didn't even crack a smile, and kept in line with the cars in front. It was hard case, man, those kids thought I was important.

Rebecca Styles

A version of this work was published in *Flash Frontier* (July 2013).

Eat beetroot

Mariana ate sliced beetroot straight from the can, as if it was a sacrament. The disc, not quite the colour of blood, dripped as she put it onto her tongue; she held it there for a moment, chewed and swallowed.

Greg came in to get his jacket. Mariana's back was straight, her dishevelled hair tumbling down. *Wispy – like baby's hair*, Greg thought. He turned and left for work.

She did not hear his goodbye, entranced by the starlings flying into the macrocarpa hedge, dry grass dangling from their beaks. They landed on the branches and disappeared into the tangle of foliage.

She ate another piece. The beetroot's strong, earthy flavour was masked, but only just, by the vinegar.

'A hamburger's only a hamburger if it's got beetroot in it,' she said. 'I've eaten a whole can. What does that make me?'

Mariana's feet were cold. She had no slippers on, only the dressing gown she'd scrambled into to go to the bathroom. In the toilet bowl was her blood. An icy slab had slammed down on her.

Ice numbed; ice froze. Ice kept things the way they were.

Would she begin to feel something? Anything? Her emotions had flown away like the starlings.

She wouldn't try and collect them yet. The thing to do was to settle. Land on a branch where it was safe.

Replenish the blood. Eat beetroot.

JANE SWAN

A version of this work was published in *Flash Frontier* (April 2014) and
Robert Olen Butler and Tara L. Masih, eds, *Best Small Fictions 2015* (Queen's Ferry Press, 2015).

Three sisters

You know how it is.
You won't open your mouth.
You won't let food in or your voice out.
Your parents say, 'Remember the starving in Africa.'

She looks okay.
She eats.
She goes to the hidden place, opens her mouth and lets it out.
She screams, but never the secret.

I study nutrition and exercise.
When I get back from the gym I shall use my new blender, which makes amazing health-giving smoothies.

There is a lost fourth child.
She ate and played, laughed and sometimes cried.

In their own ways the sisters are trying to get her back.

Jane Swan

A version of this work was published in *Flash Frontier* (December 2015).

Trip legend

Your father thinks this is a bad idea.

On this island of churches, dungarees are swimsuits. Knees scarred by fish bones are hidden behind hemlines of propriety that fall to the shins.

Naked feet shy away from shoes that arrive in tiny boxes padded with soft tissue paper. Mucus lines are wiped by the back of a hand too wild and free to recognise other uses of soft tissue paper.

A feast is thrown onto banana leaf plates. Salt mounds collapse from the landing of succulent pork flesh. Knees fold, bums anchor. Fingers reach out and convince themselves they are knives and forks – the banana leaf plates remain silent, empty of the desire to correct.

Mosquito nets are fastened to tree branches on hot sticky nights. Mothers fan their babies to sleep. Fathers lie with their clothes on spooning mothers. Their orgasms grunted into kapok pillows. Caught in the dream mats of their children.

Leave your father to me. Pack your bags.
And don't forget to borrow your brother's dungarees.

Mere Taito

That fat guy

Me, Joe and Tom were just chilling when we saw him. He was lying back on the seat, very still, with his eyes shut. 'Hey, that's that fat guy from the fish and chip shop,' I said.

'Nah,' Joe said. 'The fish shop guy had a beard.'

'It's him, I'm sure,' I said. 'He might've had a shave.' I gave the guy a prod. 'Hey, mate, giz a song – "Stairway to Heaven?"'

'Y'reckon? Why's he here then, in front of the TAB?' Joe argued. 'And not at the fish and chip shop?'

'He's not dead, is he?' Tom chipped in.

I lifted his hand. It was real cold. 'He could be dead,' I said. (*Midsomer Murders*) 'Or just asleep.'

'If he's dead, he'd be stiff as,' Joe said.

'Nah. It takes ages for that to set in,' I said. (*Crime Scene Investigation*)

I gave him another prod. 'Hey, mate, giz a song – "Stand by Me"?' Nothing. Then I noticed. 'Hey, someone must've nicked his guitar.'

'I'll check his eyes. If you're dead your eyes roll back,' I explained (*Criminal Minds*) as I lifted his eyelids. The eyes were way back.

Finally, I tried his wrist. No pulse. (*Casualty*) 'Yep, I think he's dead all right.'

'No shit,' Tom said.

'Fuck me,' Joe said.

'Come on, the pub should be open by now,' I said.

We headed off.

'I reckon it's definitely that fat guy from the fish and chip shop,' I said.

Jeff Taylor

A version of this work was published in *Flash Frontier* (June 2016).

Triptych: her shoes

On opening the mirrored white wardrobe, a waft of secret mother escapes: Coty face powder, lipstick, remnants of N°5. Unlace the twin velvet shoe bags. Small feet slide into two-tone, navy-and-white best pumps, delicate filigreed holes punched along the seams. Teetering across the bedroom carpet, dragging the shoes on outstretched toes, trying on a voice to match: 'How *do* you *do*?' Friction burns soles, guilt rising as a key clatters in the front door lock.

*

Viewed from under the table, a herd of legs mills below the chattering canopy of heads and clinking drinks. The men's pleated slacks are black or navy; their shoes standard black lace-ups, smelling of fresh Kiwi polish. They pursue peep toes, kitten heels, slingbacks, strappy white sandals with bows, mirror-shiny black patent leather. The women's stockinged legs are uniform American tan, except for one pair in seamed black fishnets sporting pointy red crocodile pumps, toes squeezed into a miniature cleavage, the heel a metal-tipped spike emitting crisp click-clacks on the parquet. Later, the crowd gone, an angry exchange is overheard:

'Stilettos! How will we ever get rid of these frightful dents?'

'But darling, I couldn't very well order a woman to take her shoes off.'

*

Her swollen feet are pressed into low-heeled, navy-blue court shoes with an ornamental buckle of conjoined silver Cs; the soles are barely scuffed. Incongruous support tights – brown, sagging, gleaming with elastane – have been paired with these trophy shoes, bought from an elegant Brussels branch of Bally, at the end of a leisurely sales process during which Madame had been offered coffee and a seat on a white sofa. Although out of place within the trappings of modern terminal care, the shoes are too ladylike to complain, and are glad for this brief, last outing.

Vivian Thonger

La Crue de la Seine, 28 Janvier 1910

The river rising through the old quarries, the underground galleries, signs of the flood on our pediments.

A bend in the river, and now the water's too slow, and it rises; its dirty line stains us.
You: *We'll be safe on the third floor* but I'm not so sure, no, I'm not so sure …

The cries of the flower sellers beneath the horse chestnuts and the white *lilas forcé*. It should not be white. It should be, well, lilac
and also peonies, the right colour peonies, and also violets

in the park that man picked a pigeon up, and cuddled and stroked it, that man picked a pigeon up
these *glaces* like flowers, each petal moulded with that strange little implement, half knife and half spoon – *au chocolat, à la fraise, à la menthe* –

by the Tuileries path, a garden disappearing: two box hedges, spiralling, the height diminishing until it descends *souterrain* as if into the underworld. Do you see? How clever whoever designed it,

how terribly

terribly

clever

and the room like an eye, all curves and water, grey and silver, and the floating flowers and the shadows of the trees and the light sent back so you've no idea what's beneath it, that dark grey/stone green water

and you feeding crumbs to sparrows, and the man dressed in green,

Granny Smith top hat and lichen shirt and grass green waistcoat, malachite trousers and moss green shoes; did you see the man dressed in green?

Upstairs, the red curtains don't seem so funny, no, they don't seem so funny. I sit by the window and look down on the careful, circular nap of top hats, their crowns so many universes, so many black holes.

Where are you?

Never here when you're needed

Never here when you're needed

EMMA TIMPANY

A version of this work was published in *Ink, Sweat and Tears* (March 2016).

Miri

'Everything is a fashion accessory,' Miri says. 'And if you don't understand that, then you are a fashion accessory.

'But don't think that it makes you fashionable.'

*

After the break-up, she finds a new boy very quickly.

'I'm going to be Frank with you,' says the boy. 'If nothing else, I'm going to be Frank.'

'You don't have to,' she tells him. 'I don't mind if you're not Frank, sometimes.'

So he stops being Frank, and starts a regime of little fibs.

Rather I fib, he thinks. Rather I fib, than be Frank.

*

Later, Miri purchases a shrink-wrap machine. She starts with food: she shrink-wraps everything in the kitchen. Then she does the books and pot plants.

Then she does the dog.

*

When Not-Frank leaves, Miri shrink-wraps their love-notes and trinkets. Later, she shrink-wraps their house, their friends, and their history.

Lots of plastic. Lots and lots of plastic.

Reuben Todd

This work was previously published in *Flash Frontier* (July 2014).

A cup of tea

After lunch my wife asked her if she would like a cup of tea, and my mother said yes, she would, if my wife was having one. No, my wife said, I'm asking if you want a cup of tea. Only if you're having one! said my mother, brightly. It's not a question of whether I'm having one, my wife said. The question is whether you want a cup of tea. Do you want one, or not? My mother, who was old, assumed a frightened look. I don't want to be any trouble, she said. I looked at my wife, but she and my mother were eyeing each other, a young woman in her own kitchen and another woman, much older. Do you want a cup of tea? my wife asked, carefully. My mother said nothing. Suddenly I felt pure hatred for my mother, and her self-negating ways. For Christ's sake, do you want a cup of tea! I shouted at her. She made no answer, but clasped her hands together and looked heavenward, like the martyrs in the framed pictures we had in our family home when I was growing up: Saint Sebastian full of arrows. This was years ago. She is dead now, my mother, and all that remains of her is buried in the ground.

Tim Upperton

This work was previously published in *The Night We Ate The Baby* (Haunui Press, 2014).

Women's studies

The alarm went off. I opened my eyes. Another day.

The little blue scooter started on the second try. I drove in and parked beneath the large neon letters. Femme Fatale.

I dragged the vacuum cleaner around the rooms, wiped down the black, vinyl-covered beds, and cleaned the hairs out of spa baths. I swiped my card and opened the door to the last room. A couple sat together on the bed, as naked and beautiful as Adam and Eve. I stared at them. They stared at me. I shut the door.

An older woman hurried down the hallway towards me, giggling.

'You'll never guess what my guy wants,' she said. 'Nappies!'

That'll be fun to clean up later, I thought.

The girls' dressing room smelt of hairspray and powder. A woman lay on the floor in the fetal position. I vacuumed around her.

I humped the Electrolux downstairs to the dark lounge, where the surfaces were reflective and fish swam pointlessly in slender tanks. Two young, nice-looking guys stood at the bar. They watched me as I worked.

'She'd do,' said one of them.

'She's more fuckable than half the girls in here,' said the other.

I finished my shift, washed my hands and went to my women's studies lecture. On the way home I spent the morning's pay on organic vegetables. I made an ethical, vegan dinner. My long-distance boyfriend called and quizzed me about my day.

I never told him about Femme Fatale. I never told him about the panic attacks.

The alarm went off. I felt the dread before I opened my eyes. Another day. Not another day.

Kathryn van Beek

That summer

Every day that summer the sky was blue. Some days it was a cloudless cartoon bubble-gum blue. Sometimes a wispy powdery blue overlaid with a delicate filigree of cirrus cloud. The days were long and hot and we swam in the sea, now placid and benign, and as warm as the Caribbean. Only a few months ago, we had cursed it – an untamed beast with hideously large cold water fins that thrashed against the shoreline, until it collapsed before our eyes, a rubble of boulder-crumbs.

We floated on our backs, eyes closed, and thought our own thoughts. *This is what summer should be. This is what it is to be young and free.* We sat in the sun in our protective neck-to-ankle bathing suits, faces smeared with SPF 100 sunscreen, eating our picnic lunches, until it was too hot to bear. Then we would return to the carpark, carefully picking our way through the now treeless promenade, over broken tarmac and patches of burnt yellow grass.

'See you tomorrow,' we called out to each other. If we said it, it would happen.

And high in that blue sky, the camera eye of a drone blinked, recording a slow procession, a caravan of SUVs like camels crossing a desert.

Latika Vasil

Winter in Auckland

Winter in Auckland. The spiralling and radiating lines of each spider web are covered by countless beads of moisture. Small and white and perfectly spaced, they hang from every strand, their collective weight causing the larger structures to sag in the middle as though they were melting in the cold. The first web I notice is suspended at the centre of a wire gate. After this, webs begin to appear in all the shrubs and bushes along the path. The more I look, the more there are, the absolute stillness of the early morning having preserved their skeletal shapes. And it strikes me that if I could somehow find a way, without breaking a single thread, to decant the dew, then the webs would become invisible again, and I would be left with several crates of bottles filled with crystal-clear liquid.

Back at home, the bushes are replaced by rows of books. I sit at my desk and listen to the words rustling between the closed pages: busy, fast, important words; words forming conclusions, proposing theories, involving themselves in metaphors and allegories; words describing old worlds, inventing new worlds, creating complex narratives that generate hundreds of characters … Sometimes my books oppress me. I reach for the *Oxford English Dictionary* - to bring the words back into line - and there, under 'dew', I find the following entry:

> *atmospheric vapour condensing in small droplets on cool surfaces*
> *between nightfall and morning.*

Perhaps dew - or the concept of dew - enabled the compilers of the dictionary to relax, to indulge in a brief dream as they fine-tuned their definitions. And I feel refreshed; I feel I can go on with words.

materialising
on a misty day –
so many spider webs

Richard von Sturmer

Peacock

'Better than guard dog!' argued Dad, swinging open the car door. From the back seat the peacock alighted, fanned its tail and strutted past us as if inspecting its troops. As it shimmied into our yard, one hundred feathered eyes like one hundred ladies-in-waiting bobbed behind. I'd wanted a Labrador.

'What eat?' demanded Maternal-Grandmother.

'Uhhh … leftovers!' lied Dad. 'Cheap!'

Maternal-Grandmother looked pointedly at me, my mate Toby, eight siblings, Auntie Lin-Lin and Uncle Huang. Mealtime at our house was like a fancy restaurant's – two sittings and a waitlist.

'Shagua,' muttered Maternal-Grandmother.

'Dumb melon,' I translated for Toby. There's no Chinese word for leftovers.

'You watch,' predicted Dad. 'With the King, we never be rob again.'

And he was right. Enthroned atop our TV antennae, the King screeched the passing of legs, wheels and wind; of sunbeams, showers and shadows; of new moons, full moons and falling stars. No threat went unheralded. Between patrols he descended only to shit on the washing or ransack the garden. Maternal-Grandmother, brandishing bunches of bruised bok choy, shouted modified Peking duck recipes at the roof.

But on moonless nights, he roosted on my bedroom window sill. He would swivel his long neck to look me right in the eye before turning his gaze to the gate. Gravediggers were banished from my dreams. Robbers were thwarted at the gate. I slept the sleep of kings.

Three months later the King proclaimed the arrival of the council ranger.

'We've received complaints about your peacock, Mr. Chien.'

'Who?' demanded Dad.

'It's unclear, sir. They're written mostly in Chinese.' Maternal-Grandmother retreated quickly to Countdown.

The King's reign was over. Perched on the back seat, waiting to be chauffeured away, he unfurled his tail. As the car departed, the King turned and one hundred and two shining eyes quivered goodbye.

Ann Webber

This work was previously published in *Flash Frontier* (July 2012).

& some scenes together

She watched him peel off his Coca-Cola T-shirt in the filthy apartment opposite her own. After he changed and left, she split in two, making a whispering sound like an eggplant parting into a pair of foamy white kidneys. The shine of the split throbbed; it hurt her first self's eyes, made her scrunch up her fists.

Her second self cut her hair. She was blithe and laughed a lot, mimicking the movements of the impatient dog walker she could feel pacing on the pavement outside. Taking handfuls of it, she cradled the dark strands in her right palm, twitching. The scissors were blunt, so she used toenail clippers. It was slow. It gave her a look like stairs ascending.

One of them coaxed the other into attending, boldly picking up a flyer after class. Hands were clasped, voices gaily sang, and their bellies gasped from too many hot dogs. *A glimpse of a Coca-Cola T-shirt wittered into view, but it was orange, not black, and flew through the crowd twitching, like a chalky-grey moth at dusk.* One of them sneezed loudly from the pollen. They briefly wondered if they had spent their time well and what that meant.

Afterwards, the line of cedars waving along the street looked different. She thought it could be a spareness. Perhaps even a wallowing.

Elizabeth Welsh

A version of this work was published in *Flash Frontier* (February 2015).

The sadness of gifts

A man saw his wife wrapped as a Christmas present. The wind picked up their tent, slipping each guy-rope, and bundled her away. In another instant she returned to earth, the pivot on which she spun. The tent did not consent to fly. The wind did not seek permission. The man begged the wind to be gentle.

The wind was flagrant. It caught her hair and smashed her down. It ran at yachts and cracked them like a whip on their moorings. The man found his wife in the limp wreckage of the tent. He heard the sea protest. He felt twigs pull at his hair. He fumbled at zippers. The fabric held tight, his broken Christmas present as if all life had ebbed away. Still the wind tugged at them, urging him to play.

A man saw his wife wrapped in wind. He was dashed if he could remember anything more than that. There were pegs in the ground. The ground had cheated him, giving her leave to fly away. She had never thought to fly. He cursed his thought of it, that dreams had taught the wind this thing.

Tom Weston

This work was previously published in *Small Humours of Daylight* (Steele Roberts, 2008).

Traffic noise

Make no mistake. The delicacy of the horn is a porcelain vase, its rage a gun that shoots its victims down. It is *yes* with a dozen meanings, the *yes* of *no*, the *yes* of *maybe*, an almanac, the shudder of love and the shout of the policeman, the bearer of drinks. The horn is the tongue of the road, insolent and hard in what it takes, a singer that can assume any damn lyric.

It is a black choir, a choir of boys in a cathedral, the Pope as he blesses a crowd, white with flecks of gold and purple. A low noise, calculating. The horn resists an answer. It drives a long way for you. *Yes* and *no* muster a discordant tune. The horn is rules made in an instant, details etched in the eardrum's cells, insistent you are nothing more than here.

It is the day as it becomes smaller about you, abandoned everywhere, marked with incomprehension, announcements in a foreign tongue, how to buy food, what to expect. The horn reduces to these simple things and it drains you. The querulous tongue is one of complaint, of imminent argument, where threats are the taking of territory and a refusal to see the consequences.

The couple in the taxi queue has been wounded. She is blotched with iodine and his arm is in plaster. The horn does not care. They find a car and she lifts their case into the boot. Pain burns them. An Egyptian drives through the city. He understands the pattern of bruises like a roadmap. His English is halting but he finds where each one leads. This is the tongue and the taking, every step retraced.

Tom Weston

This work was previously published in *Small Humours of Daylight* (Steele Roberts, 2008).

The freeloaders

Flat Cap was looking out the window, contemplating. Today's fellow travellers were the usual assortment. Sonia – she cultivated people knowing her name – was sitting next to Walking Stick, who earlier had done her assisted sprint from the feeder bus. The Crusher had found a seat to himself, to everyone's relief. Placemaker Man was sitting behind the driver. Blue Coat (who actually hadn't worn it for a year) had chosen Flat Cap to sit next to today – she never sat next to the same person two days running. Other passengers from the later stops seized the remaining seats. It was as if the freeloaders had been waiting for this to happen, or because the air in the bus had reached wing-muscle temperature. Or maybe, with their acute sense of hearing, they had heard Iggy Pop singing through Flat Cap's string phones. Whatever it was, when the cicadas started stirring on the floor of the bus the effect was electric. The Crusher turned pale and gripped his knees, conversations erupted between previously mute companions, men and women lowered their faces in consternation and tried to brush any flying freeloaders away. Blue Coat calmly pulled a tissue from her purse, leant down and gathered up a couple of crawlers. She handed it to Flat Cap and pointed at the open top window. Eventually all were dispatched one way or another. Iggy Pop, the iconic rocker who sometimes sang live dressed only in his undies, was still singing his punk anthem – The Passenger. 'Oh the passenger, He rides and He rides, He looks through his window, what does he see?' belted through Flat Cap's string phones. He was sure now the cicadas had only wanted to join in the riff. Iggy Pop and the Cicadas – that would have been something.

KEITH WESTWATER

This work was previously published in *Felt Intensity* (Submarine imprint, Mākaro Press, 2015).

Slow day in skunkworks

It starts like this: I knock over my thermos and it takes a full hour to hit the ground. The rhizome-like spread of coffee takes another hour. That's how I know. A slow day.

It's midday before the mess is cleaned. These conditions are unsuitable for thought. I've complained. Sent memos. Contacted Adams in Space/Time monitoring. He says the thingy's broke. An expensive patch is needed. I just have to deal. So I deal. I try and think, but no bubbles reach the surface.

Only one thought comes: *The food was pureed then rectally infused.* I don't know this thought. It isn't one of mine. I cannot shake it.

Nonetheless, I record it. It's a struggle. After 45 minutes, my pen hits paper. Another 30 minutes and I've crossed the T. It's beyond silly.

A memo comes. I'm behind schedule. Demands unmet. Risking expulsion. I consider replying, but it's futile. I memo Adams instead. He says he can't perform repairs. Says I ought to find a solution. I'm the thinking man, aren't I? Yes, but thought is too slow here. *The food was pureed then rectally infused.* Doesn't help. All I've got.

I spend hours twiddling thumbs, bending paperclips. To no end. One thought like a mantra. Useless. Nonsense. A thoughtless thinking man.

All day, no other thoughts, then one comes like a face out of fog. It's unbearably sad.

Brendon Stanton White

This work was previously published in *Flash Frontier* (April 2016).

Ophelia at Huntly

She was stumbling back from the pub, singing, cursing, crying. No need to hurry home, now Dad was dead and Joey doing a long stretch up at Paremoremo.

Orange streetlight dripped onto the road and, in the distance, a siren sounded the shift change. She stopped on the bridge for a quiet smoke. Morning glory climbed the railings, its violet trumpets throbbing in the darkness. She reached over to touch a velvet bloom. Over and down.

And then the water, surprisingly warm, welcoming even. She didn't struggle; she let it take her under.

The river entwined her in its sinuous limbs, embraced her, and caressed her with its slippery fingers. Lithe and serpentine, it slid into her mouth and between her thighs. She was coming and drowning at the same time.

No one would know whether she'd jumped or fallen. Was she flotsam or jetsam? She didn't know. The river didn't care. But it would keep her safe – safe from the drinking and the drudgery, the hidings and the hurting, the pricks and the fists. The river wouldn't grow tired of her or reject her. It was her one true lover. She wanted to lie in its silten-silken bed forever, sleeping in the warm darkness – floating beyond time – watched over by the sad-eyed catfish while the watery stars wheeled above.

*

They found her amongst the other debris at Intake No. 4: plastic bottles, polystyrene, old jandals, a supermarket trolley. Her dress wound in a tight shroud around her body, rotting raupō in her hair.

As they prised her away from the grating, she rolled on her back and floated for a moment, arms outstretched, blank face to the wide Waikato sky. The police diver thought she reminded him of someone, but he couldn't think who.

Sian Williams

This work was previously published in *Flash Frontier* (August 2016).

Bones

These bones remind me of the time you stayed in a hut at Hakatere Beach and knitted a raw wool jersey for my birthday. Two months later you shot through to Auckland.

Last Easter I drove down to Hakatere Beach. I wondered about you being there alone when you were only seventeen. The huts were deserted. The beach was cold and bleak and windswept. I didn't hang around. I put a dead shag in a plastic bag and took it home. I buried it in a terracotta pot with a handful of tiger worms.

This Easter I dug the dead bird up. The feathers and flesh were completely gone. Only this scatter of bones remained. Sleek, ochre bones; each one quite beautiful. I washed them in warm water and bleach and here they are in front of me in a white plastic ice cream container.

Nicholas Williamson

A version of this work was published in *The Blue Outboard: New and Selected Poems* (Black Doris Press, 2016).

Hands

Outside it is quieter.

I lower myself onto a wooden bench. Its silver skin matches the concrete below. I finger the grooves. When will I see green again?

My hands just did things that were wrong.

I think back to the day I left the house – in a storm.

The wind was high-pitched against the windows and it almost unravelled me. I knew what was to come. As I dressed that morning, the belt on the bed reminded me of things I'd rather forget. My scraped knuckles stood out proud, beyond the rings that adorned them.

No rings in here.

Before I closed the door I paused, like a bird waiting for a worm to turn the soil below. I looked out towards the rock at the harbour mouth that had always reminded me of a humpback whale. In calm seas the waves soothed it.

There is no such relief for me.

In the storm that day, I heard the struggle between leaf and tree, a desperate embrace to stay attached to one another. Like her and me.

My thoughts are interrupted.

'Got a smoke, mate?'

'Sure,' I say. There's no point saying otherwise. I'm a bottom-feeder now.

'Gets pretty noisy at mealtimes, eh?' he says to me.

I nod.

'You were a legend back in the day. The way you'd dance in the ring. Man, I used to wish I was you,' he said.

I dip my head, and stand up to face him.

IONA WINTER

This work was previously published in *Flash Frontier* (February 2016).

Calligraphy

Around ten to three we gather in chatty groups outside the classroom. He never joins us. He takes up a position to one side, alone. He pulls a paperback from his jacket pocket. He adjusts the Mandarin collar around his nape, lowers his capped head, and reads. He reads vertical lines that from a distance look like bird claws. His face is steep and still, his expression sorrowful. There are scoops of shadow in the fall of flesh beneath his cheekbones.

One day I arrive early. The playground is deserted. No, he's there, squatting in the middle of the netball court, peering into a puddle of rainwater. He holds an artist's paintbrush. He dips the brush in the puddle. A trail of claw marks appears on the asphalt. Each glistens for a few seconds, dulls and vanishes. The thin brush moves deliberately and delicately, but quickly, quick as a heron stepping through an estuary in pursuit of butterfish. Quick as a poet with a caught shoal of words.

He lifts his clay-cliff face. Although it is completely silent, and there is nothing to be seen on the netball court except an old man now carefully pocketing a paintbrush, birds are lifting off the surface in their thousands. I hear a beat-rush flurry, warning cries.

I look away.

*

After the bell, my daughter and his granddaughter emerge from their classroom, head to head, giggling. He's standing to one side, eyes on his book. My daughter glances up. '*Nihau, Mr Young*!' she sings.

Some small winged moment passes between them, sets loose from him the slightest of nods. His granddaughter skips over and takes his hand. He leads her out, across the netball court, across that wide, quiet delta, its evaporated claw-talk, all its birds in flight.

Sue Wootton

A version of this work was published in *Flash Frontier* (August 2016).

Votive

Bobby watched the television news. Massacres and earthquakes, any tragedy really, and out with the candles. Where did they all come from, and what did people think candles could do? You could bet your bottom dollar people weren't taking them from their emergency kits. Most people didn't keep an emergency kit. Maybe they thought that when *their* earthquake struck, when *their* massacre happened, the candles amassing in a multitude of town squares across the planet would enable them to see in the dark. Back in the shattered place, Bobby meant. Back under the collapse, with the broken bones and the broken plumbing and the complete absence of power. But these weren't *that* kind of candle, the emergency kit Seven Hour Burn kind. These were mostly tea candles, votive flames.

And suddenly there was her father walking into the picture with a wreath. His expression was solemn, just right for the occasion. He had dressed casually for this one, Levi's and black polo neck. These must be clothes picked out for him by his newest wife, who was Arty. *Ha*! thought Bobby, who remembered how scathing her father had always been about art. No, not about art (he liked to purchase good pieces), about artists. Because they were slackers, always looking for a handout. They didn't *work*.

He was working: he laid the wreath against the railings, and picked up someone's candle. Bobby had been well into her teens before she realised that they weren't called vote candles, those ones in the church that he would light on Sundays. Now, seeing him so reverent, sad and honourable by candlelight, she thought, *Well, who could blame me for making that mistake for so long*?

Sue Wootton

Two fish

She asked questions that simultaneously were too personal, and sounded as if she had found them in a how-to manual.

'So, what was your childhood like?'

> *Everyone likes talking about themselves! Ask open questions about his friends, family, and hobbies.*

'Siblings?'

> *Asking about his family relationships will help you to reach his more emotional side, and give you some insight into what to expect!*

'Oo, brothers. I bet you fought.'

He liked her kind, grey eyes though, and the sleek smallness of her in the aquamarine dress.

'What's your brother like?'

He tried stalling, took another glass of wine. This was a mistake. The crystal glass stood no chance against his quaking, oversized hands.

The moment before it smashed he saw two angel fish suspended in the golden liquid, opening and closing their mouths. And while the waiter fussed, he remembered when his brother kicked a soccer ball through the wall of his tropical aquarium. He had rushed to scoop the fish into pots filled with water from the kitchen. Many died from the shock of the temperature change. Their scales shimmered iridescent colours as they died, while his small boy's heart turned to glass and shattered. Others were cut by the glass as they spilled onto the carpet, and swam in distressed circles in cooking pots of their own dilute blood.

The waiter evaporated. So did the date. Well-dressed people opened and closed their mouths. He searched the wine stain and the shards for the angel fish and decided, again, not to call his brother.

Phoebe Wright

Esmé and the whitebait

It so happened the day it rained whitebait Esmé had her frying pan on the stovetop. The pan was sizzling with butter for an omelette.

The sky, which had been blue when Esmé hung out the washing, changed to silver. When the whitebait came down like sleet she walked outside and held the hot pan out at arm's length. The translucent wee fish were cooked by the time she sat at the table. Birds arrived in great flocks within minutes and ate all the remaining sprats. Not a scrap of evidence was left.

Esmé's instinct was not to mention her catch to anyone, particularly her husband of many years. Austin didn't like whitebait anyway. He thought their tiny black eyes were staring at him. (Austin had his own set of tiny black eyes.)

Way back, when they were wealthy and delicate morsels of all kinds were affordable, Esmé had offered to cut the eyes off his whitebait. But he said, quite rightly, there wouldn't be enough left for a meal.

As Esmé wiped her plate with a piece of bread she thought about her father, Andy. He was a baiter with his own stand at a river mouth. His enormous net was made of white silk. His wife, Avis, Esmé's mother, had made it out of her wedding dress. Whitebait were plentiful then, so Andy brought home bucketsful of the wriggling spawn. The family soon tired of eating them and fed them to the hens.

If only her parents were alive! They would have enjoyed the story of her unexpected lunch. But they were long gone and Esmé had married the wrong man. Nothing out of the ordinary ever happened to Austin. He had no reason to believe in miracles.

LOUISE WRIGHTSON

ES

S

YS

‘What am I reading?’
Allan Drew

In the early days of Twitter (2009), *The Times* UK ran a Twitter fiction contest. The contest’s judge, the novelist and comedian David Baddiel, made an example of this entry:

> Can anyone tell me where the ‘hash’ AKA ‘pound’ symbol is on a MacBook?

Although this entry was likely to be from someone who had ‘wandered on to the wrong page’ Baddiel reserved the right for this tweet to be considered ‘a very, very clever postmodern story.’[1] And, if you’re not careful, you too will find yourself parsing the sentence for its ability to lay bare certain Signs and Truths of human existence. What I think this shows is that flash fiction is, at its heart, slippery. I want to draw attention to this slipperiness – to highlight some of the ways in which flash works, or appears to work, both with and against the narrative and lyrical norms of conventional storytelling. In other words, to throw some light on why it is that, like Baddiel back in 2009, you’re never quite sure what you’re reading when you’re reading flash.

Oscar Wilde reportedly said, ‘The only thing to do with good advice is to pass it on; it is never of any use to oneself.’ Notwithstanding this aphorism, there do seem to be some established pieces of advice for good writing: avoid clichés, and favour direct, fresh and active language. Perhaps the king of rules is *show, don’t tell.* D. R. Jones’s story in this anthology is an example of flash fiction that successfully transgresses this rule – or seems to.[2] Jones’s title, ‘Connections: a New Zealand novel in 224 words’, sets up his story as a sort of literary oxymoron (with a hint of critique, surely, of the concept of a ‘New Zealand novel’). The fiction includes such sentences as:

> Ake used to eel in Ōhāriu where his hīnaki got so full it dragged him under … Lily rows her clinker on the Mahurangi harbour … Jemima suffers from premature menopause … Garry drives a truck; takes pills to stay awake and pills to sleep …

Each sentence is a model of telling, a list of facts manifesting as summary. And yet this summary-story is satisfying as a piece of prose. Why? Or, better still, how? Part of the power of Jones's fiction lies in each sentence presenting, initially, as *telling*, before transforming, almost imperceptibly, into *showing*. Take this sentence: 'Tanya flies model planes because her dad won't let her study to be a pilot like he was.' The first four words are mere fact, and the remainder of the sentence is, similarly, fact. It *feels* like telling. However, the fact of flying model planes is critically – and emotionally – modified by the reason for Tanya flying them; by the *because*. By the time the sentence is done, we sense injustice, longing – perhaps cruelty – without these abstractions having been uttered. What first seems to be telling is, in fact, a deft act of showing. This sentence would qualify as a piece of flash on its own.

Jones has his way with this method repeatedly. In the line, 'Brendan sleeps under a bridge and turns tricks for repressed men', the word 'repressed' problematises the moment of telling. We come to learn something about Brendan/Ake – that his clientele are specifically 'repressed' men. I wonder: are they *exclusively* repressed men? Would he refuse to provide his services to *empowered* men? Does Brendan target repressed men because they are simpler clients? Or because he wants to exploit them? Or, possibly, because he feels sorry for them? This ambiguity affords Ake/Brendan the sort of psychological depth that we need to care about him. We must note too that the word 'repressed' also helps characterise Garry. Only through the characterisation of Brendan/Ake do we learn that Garry, the truck driver, is repressed (he has to be because Brendan only turns tricks for repressed men). Repressed is a short-cut word, a telling word, but deployed so that it functions as showing, and we don't object to it. Rather than keeping the reader distant, this act of telling draws us in. There are several other instances of single words or short phrases that 'pop' in this story in the same way as 'repressed'. 'Ostentatious' brings us in close to Lily's mind in a moment of free indirect discourse; 'another human' provides perhaps the opposite, a sort of dramatic irony at the expense of Jemima and John; 'indelicately' (an adverb – the most hated of all the word types in creative writing classes for their graceless *telling* function) complicates rather than simplifies the phrase 'remind her'. With Jones's story what we *think* we are reading is not, in fact, what we're reading. It's slippery.

I assert that we often *feel* poetry when we *read* flash fiction. The terms flash fiction and prose poetry are often used interchangeably, and there is little to visually distinguish a short piece of fiction from a poem written without line breaks. The boundary between them is semipermeable, translucent. It might be a matter of shifting the needle: allow it to lean more towards narrative and you have flash fiction;

allow it more lyrical freedom and you have prose poetry. Or, to put it from a writer's point of view, flash fiction affords prose writers an excuse to write lyrically, while it affords poets a way to temporarily free themselves from the tyranny of lineation.

When we read Sarah Jane Barnett's 'Lullaby',[3] we put ourselves at the mercy of a poet while thinking we're reading fiction. And we *are* reading fiction – there is narrative, there are characters, there is progression – and the piece is *visually* prose. But the story has, too, that sensuousness and music we crave from poems. The flow of, 'The radio tells me it is snowing somewhere south' is slowed, expertly and deliberately, by the 'Drifts fall down for days', with the soft alliterations mimicking the fall of snowdrops. The piece is infused with satisfying ambiguity; it unbalances the reader; nothing is certain. The ambiguity exists in observations: someone 'must have' died – but have they actually? The woman is 'neighbourly, *maybe*', and she '*tries* for lightness'. It's snowing '*somewhere* south'. But the ambiguity exists, too, in pure language. The neighbour's eyes are 'purpled' – perhaps by make-up, perhaps through exhaustion, perhaps violence – and this purpling is linked, somehow, to the woman's neighbourliness. By the time this brief story reaches its rising action, that of the woman's memory of trying (although, of course, 'you never really can') to explain grief, the reader is primed for devastation, and suitably devastated. If flash fiction is a form that will make you wonder what you're reading, then Barnett's piece typifies this.

Flash fiction can provoke a reader through its peculiar ability to engage with multiple and varied genres. The demands of very short fiction allow it the privilege of taking literary short-cuts to promote faster access to a story's emotional centre. One short-cut already discussed is that of 'telling'. Manoeuvring through different genres within a single piece of flash is another way to access meaning quickly. (Here I use the term 'genre' broadly, to mean a style common to certain categories of literature.) Zoë Meager's 'Sharp stars' recalls a number of different genre influences.[4] The effect begins in the very first lines, which have something of a fairy-tale quality about them. The simplicity of language, the lists, the repetition, the matter-of-fact construction of scene, and the recognisable scenario (trapped in a dilemma) are all tropes of fairy tales. The second paragraph, however, is a single sentence of 65 words, and breaks from this genre:

> She puts it on her youngest but her youngest slips through, and on the middle child, but the middle child slips through, so her eldest accepts it when the sea is calm and it clings to him while the sea boils and the youngest child is cut from his mother's arms, and the middle child is cut from his mother's arms by the raging world.

Meager's rhythms echo the iterative, compounding lyricism of the Bible, such as Genesis 5:2, 'So God created man in his image, in the image of God created he him; male and female created he them.' Each phrase builds on the previous and creates a sense of momentum – of purpose and significance. Meager's next line shifts the influence further: 'The sea spits out the hearts of ghosts' feels gothic, surreal, symbolic. The accumulation of these generic influences permits the ongoing use of language and tropes common and familiar in these genres, allowing Meager to hit pure notes with dramatic adjectives and high abstractions, such as 'raging world' and 'wretchlings'. The ultimate effect is that this story, contained so tightly within its frame of 294 words, can reach fearlessly and successfully outwards, to ask the really big questions posed by literature: 'where are the codes to unlock the world?' Where, indeed. Much as we might question whether we're immersed in fiction or poetry with Barnett's 'Lullaby', in Meager's story we are captured in a world whose rules keep shifting underneath us, a world in which the narrative moves between literary paradigms with such confidence that we cannot help but be taken along.

The final example of flash's slipperiness I want to touch on is the form's unapologetic and direct engagement with conceptualisation – with *ideas*. Stories in service of ideas do of course exist, and novels like Orwell's *Nineteen Eighty-Four* remain classics. Nevertheless, it remains dogmatic in the halls of creative writing schools that your stories must be in service of their characters, that the plot arises (or at least appears to arise) organically. Again, flash refuses to be restricted by these parameters – or, instead, leverages these restrictions for literary benefit. In Melanie Dixon's 'Schrödinger's cat',[5] the story immediately engages with an idea: the famous thought experiment posed by the Austrian physicist Erwin Schrödinger to model quantum mechanics. In the experiment, a (figurative) cat is placed in a box according to certain conditions, in which the cat can be thought of as both simultaneously alive and dead until the box is opened. By invoking Schrödinger's thought experiment, Dixon is able to immediately pose questions related to the problem – those of uncertainty, life and death, knowability, and so on. After all, the cat is lying there, 'contemplating the meaning of life and death'. This invocation, then, is another example of a literary short-cut to meaning. And the remainder of the story develops that idea by flicking continually between opposing alternatives. Is Erwin coming home, or not? The cat wonders about the consequences of observation – a concern to science, insofar that the mere fact of observing a phenomenon *changes* the phenomenon. This manifests in a quite quotidian way in the story, through the cat's concern that the act of looking outside will cause Erwin an injury. The success of this act lies, to some degree, in the brevity that binds flash fiction. We would, I think, quite rightly reject a longer story that pursued this thread: flash fiction's brevity, then, is integral to meaning.

My mother-in-law has on her coffee table a book of New Zealand short fiction. The contents page is a roll-call of established writers, and the stories are uniformly accomplished. The thing is, one glance at the contents page and you know, more or less, exactly what to expect. Open the contents page of *this* anthology, however, and you have no idea what's coming. The stories come at you directly, and then turn askance, and then slap you in the face. We come across fiction that looks like poetry, and poetry that looks like fiction. We're taken on tours through literary genres in fewer than 300 words, and we're asked to conceptualise in the middle of abrupt, non-realistic narratives. And in all cases, the brevity facilitates meaning and enjoyment. These stories are slippery, and exciting.

---

1 'Twitter: David Baddiel sifts through early entries in *The Times* microstory contest. At best, they are modern haikus. But don't telegraph the punchline', *The Times*, London, 3 October 2009.

2 D. R. Jones, 'Connections: a New Zealand novel in 224 words', *Bonsai*, CUP, Christchurch, 2018.

3 Sarah Jane Barnett, 'Lullaby', *Bonsai*, CUP, Christchurch, 2018.

4 Zoë Meager, 'Sharp stars', *Bonsai*, CUP, Christchurch, 2018.

5 Melanie Dixon, 'Schrödinger's cat', *Bonsai*, CUP, Christchurch, 2018.

On misunderstanding, masquerade and the prose poem

Joan Fleming

I like poems best because they try to say what is unspeakable, but among my fears is the worry that I have wasted years of my life trying to say why, when all I need to know about it, I have already said in this sentence. For a while I only wrote prose poems. The little boxes pleased me, and I wanted to be (mostly) faithful to the sentence. My careful (though wildering) logic of phrase against phrase needed that tight paragraph to generate maximal excitement.[1] Also, I wanted to be a kind of witch: inveigling a reader into the dense woods of the form (how like prose this Thing looks!) before she realises she is reading poetry. Such powers I would sometimes ascribe to myself, because writing is lonely and crazy-making.

Poets choose their forms for inexplicable reasons, and then write craft essays to legitimise their dream logic. This always fails, and must. As Frank O'Hara says, 'you just go on your nerve'. Such justifications are only a vehicle for quietening fear. Something is really happening here, we say to ourselves. The dark swimming of composition is a thing that can be talked about in the daytime. When we explain it, we kill it sometimes. There is an idea that after Jesus died, the first generation of Christians cherished a potent symbol for the church: the body of Christ. Christ *was* the church, and the Mystic Body was the way to crystallise that feeling. All believers were part of this body, a body that was metaphorical, supernatural, mysterious. The body of Christ suggested the unspeakable joy of being in Jesus' presence – of, well, feeling the love. Then when mass proselytising required that the church be systematised, this symbol acquired a confounding logic: the body of Christ was explained as being both fully human and fully divine; Christ was divided and conjoined into both *one* and *three*. These paradoxes became scaffolded by generations and generations of what we call Theology. Thus the mystic poetry of religious experience is smothered by the justifications of the head. My favourite essays (*essai*: a trial) are the ones that keep their doors ajar, in order to avoid such smothering. I like them to perpetuate the impossible expectations we have for poetry: that poems must be both deeply mysterious and able to be ciphered; that poems must sing divine universals with a profane and particular voice; that poems must be both uselessly aesthetic and politically expedient. I like the motion of this perpetuation, and I like its crash back to earth.

It is the province of prose to turn wonderings and discomforts into knowledge-possession. Would baking soda get this tarnish off? What precipitated the wrongness of our mental environment? Who elected this man, and where can I emigrate? It is to prose that we can take our questions. Prose gives us instruction, analysis, cause and effect.

It is to poetry, however, that we can take our cravings for a dreamy brain-spark that makes familiar things strange again.

One of the best tricks of the prose poem is that it can masquerade as a prose form we might approach for information. For example, the business memo:

> Understand that we will be working together / and this means / we do not have to like each other. / Understand that we have common goals / and aspirations, we have aspirations / most of all. / Understand, that in the end, / the unspoken is always spoken / and usually by someone not qualified to speak it. Understand, / the rhythm of this agreement is not always symmetric, / sometimes the drummer starts to lean / on one thigh, slowly sags to the side, / and as a result the song can sound like mud and honey. / Understand, that I love you. / Understand, that this doesn't necessarily concern you. / Understand, that this is a bridging agreement, / just a place-holder / until the full programme of individual projects that need to occur to realise the full potential of the programme which addresses all the individual and specific concerns and develops a full and proper understanding of all the aforementioned concerns / is in place. Understand, / that there are no place-holders.
>
> (Bill Nelson, *Memorandum of Understanding,* excerpt)[2]

Or the letter:

> Susan performed one song and I must confess, I was taken aback. I had always thought her talent fairly pedestrian, but you would not believe the improvements she has made this past summer. She has somehow trained her voice to be very full, almost erotically voluminous, like hydrangeas, if that means to you what it does for me. The best I could muster was a borrowed duet, which actually was a great deal of fun although there was a bad moment when Esther did not know where I was. I had told her after the chorus we would go straight to the bridge, but she must not have heard me and by the time we found each other she was sobbing and I was panicking and calling out and darling, I really do not know what I would have done next.
>
> (Louise Wallace, 'Darling')[3]

Notice in Mr Nelson's poem, the appropriation of corporate jargon and its reluctant bedfellow, the stock-standard love declaration. I haven't quoted the whole poem, but the whole poem is wonderful, especially the end, where he gets to the 'wobbly bits' and squeezes them. Here we have agreements, place-holders, aforementioned concerns, and wobbly bits, all sharing space. The poem makes the familiar formulation 'I love you' complicated and weird. We don't expect to stumble upon it in a memo. Cheerfully grotesque human frailty and the comforts of shared bodies are grafted onto the hard distancing of memo-speak.

Ms Wallace also uses the device of apostrophe, the literary mode of direct address to a person not present. Again, the formulations are familiar, if old-timey: 'I must confess'; 'you would not believe'; 'The best I could muster'; 'a great deal of fun'. We've seen these sorts of letters before, maybe in our grandparents' archives. We know where we are, don't we, readers? Until we get to Susan's voice blooming like 'erotically voluminous … hydrangeas'. Ms Wallace is pulling a sneaky trick on us, and when we arrive at the 'bridge', the bridge is bigger than it is, more consequential, more vibrational. The bridge is the location of panic, the fear of losing someone dear, and the choked-up joy of reunion. The fact that 'Darling' is dedicated to the poet Rachel Bush, who died the year it was published, makes the irony of the poem's reunion all the more bittersweet.

I suspect we are most of us quite good at masquerading as immortals. We make our doomed little plans and pretend that death is something that happens to other people. I, for one, pretend every day to be a capable grown-up, but truth be told I go stupid with fear if I pause to seriously consider, say, a loveless old age, or the tearing body of childbirth, or the black collapse of ecosystems. A square of poetry – a tidy, rational-looking paragraph shape that knows where its edges are – is as good a place as any to get healingly absurd.

Robert Frost said a poem should start in delight and end in wisdom. This is a solid formula, but an old one. Some poems that do great and helpful things start in instruction, and end in bewilderment. Like this one:

> I think you need to paint a bit of blue between the legs. For there is blue beyond the legs, and blue beyond the body, and there's blue beyond the head, and there is blue beyond the blue eyes, softly gazing out. Only, there is no out. No on beyond the eyes, or eye-lashes, no on beyond the head, the neck, the back, the legs, the spots. You cannot take away the head, the neck, you cannot take away the legs, the spots, you cannot take away an eyelash, not a single one, and not the single back, and not the bit of blue between the legs because there is no bit of blue between the legs.
>
> (Anna Jackson, 'A sonnet about a giraffe')[4]

What?! Exactly. What, indeed. For one thing, this is no sonnet. I am being lied to.[5] And I begin by thinking, yes, a bit of blue between the legs – good idea! That will make everything lifelike. By the end, I don't know what blue is, or where it's found, or how to conceive of this giraffe of words. And I need to go back and read the poem again from the beginning. That is how Charles Simic, a great sorcerer of the form, defines the prose poem: 'What makes them poems is that they are self-contained, and once you read one you have to go back and start reading it again. That's what a poem does.'

Now I am worried this essay is turning into some sort of treatise on what prose poems can and cannot do. In writing we are sometimes our own worst nightmare.

One smart thing I am doing, though, is to abstain from talking about prose poems that are narratives, or at least have some kind of narrative cohesion, like the sequences in Sarah Jane Barnett's *Work*, or Gregory Kan's *This Paper Boat*, or Zarah Butcher-McGunnigle's *Autobiography of a Marguerite*, all of which are incredible, and all of which I will leave to those who understand how story works. My subject, the self-contained paragraph, continues to elude me, but I will keep talking about it anyway.

Obviously, many, many prose poems are the relatives of dreams, because dreams are where our psychic rubbish, our aspirations and our anxieties, get all mashed up and eerie and prophetic on us: 'Last night a woman offered to give me an injection against crossness and frustration' – Hannah Mettner, 'Sex Dream'; 'I feel things happening around me that are not real. I must be in a dream' – Nina Powles, 'Miyazaki Bloom'; 'I dream of you in a white tuxedo. It is a wedding. It is not our wedding. But the face that you affix to yourself when you look into me is the face of the man viewing the woman. Hello this is love.' – Emma Barnes, 'White Tuxedo.' It is kind to announce the poem as a Dream Poem in the first line, or in the title, though many don't. This is partly where the prose poem gets its reputation as a surreal form. It is said that in a word-association game, the prompt 'prose poem' would be followed by the association 'surreal' or 'surrealism'.[6] Perhaps after reading this essay, other things might come to mind, like 'body of Christ' or 'giraffe', both of which would be wrong, and therefore right.

Prose poems are also good for attempted self-definition ('The phasing we are together is a waveform where I am the peak and you are the valley. We are edge to edge like all good risks and measures' – Emma Barnes, 'Give Up') where the appropriated language of science or commerce lends a grown-up air to the investigation, which is only play. You might take issue with my alignment of the prose poem to kid activities. You might well. The truth is, writing of this kind is *not* work proper. It is labour of a kind that, by and large, ruling politicians and parent-figures still counselling us to apply our creative powers to achieve success in the business sector in order to build a life that Makes Sense cannot understand.[7]

Not that the poets themselves understand any better. This is what I am trying to say, and saying badly, but musically. There is a reason all good poets stammer when they're asked by non-poets 'What kind of poetry do you write?' What kind of poetry *is* there? My name is Rachel O'Neill and I write surreal vignettes. My name is Frankie McMillan and I write tiny stories. To answer this question earnestly is to begin giving an awkward lesson on *what poetry is* to someone who (usually) doesn't really care. Better, perhaps, that poets keep talking to other poets about the things they all realise can never be known. Shouting into the caves. Murmuring better questions into tide-marked Wedgewood. Making faces in the mirror, recognising ourselves as monkeys, old women, fractious babies, felons and ghosts.

---

1 The term 'maximal excitement' owes something to Lyn Hejinian, who writes: 'In the "open text" … all the elements of the work are maximally excited … because ideas and things exceed (without deserting) argument.' See 'The Rejection of Closure', Poetry Foundation, accessed 30 October 2017 from https://www.poetryfoundation.org/articles/69401/the-rejection-of-closure.

2 Bill Nelson, *Memorandum of Understanding*, VUP, Wellington, 2016.

3 Louise Wallace, 'Darling', *Bad Things*, VUP, Wellington, 2017.

4 Anna Jackson, 'A sonnet about a giraffe', *Sport 41*, 2013.

5 Actually, the paragraph is a sort of introduction to a fourteen-line and therefore sonnet-like *something* called 'Giraffe' whose first line is: 'I think you need to paint a little bit of blue between the legs.'

6 David Lehman says this in his introduction to *Great American Prose Poems: From Poe to the Present*. He writes, 'Someone quipped that if you said prose poem in a word association game the next word to come to everybody's mind would be *surrealist* or *surreal*.' David Lehman, *Great American Prose Poems: From Poe to the Present*, Scribner, New York, 2003, p. 20.

7 This idea of work vs. labour is indebted to Lewis Hyde's wonderful book *The Gift: Creativity and the Artist in the Modern World*, Penguin Random House, New York, 2007.

Walls and bridges
Tim Jones

Borders and boundaries are uppermost in many minds, from the tangerine in the White House to those charged with patrolling, enforcing and crossing them. It's hard to get away from boundaries when discussing small fictions, because a central question of the field is how to locate the boundary between what is, and what isn't, a small fiction.

But it's not just one border – or if it is, it's a border that exists in several dimensions at once. One of those dimensions is length: just how short is short enough to include? The answer varies:

- *Flash Frontier*: max 250 words.
- NZ's National Flash Fiction Day competition: max 300 words.
- *Bonsai*: max 300 words.
- The very successful late 1990s–early 2000s series of New Zealand short short story anthologies edited by Graeme Lay, and later Graeme Lay and Stephen Stratford: max 500 words.
- The annual *Best Small Fictions* anthology series (series editor Tara L. Masih) sets both an upper and lower limit: 1000 words and 6 words respectively.[1]

The range is remarkable. A 1000-word limit imposes very different constraints to a 250-word limit. That's four times as many words!

But there's another constraint to consider: what is, and is not, fiction? It's pretty easy to tell the difference between a prose poem and *War and Peace*, but when the prose poem and the piece of fiction are of equal length, and formatted the same way, how do we tell one from the other – and does it even matter?

The work selection for *Bonsai* signals the close relationship of prose poetry and small fiction. In looking at both new and previously published works to recommend for consideration, I came to the conclusion that there is no hard and fast distinction that separates one from the other: it's often simply a matter of where they are first published, or how the author defines the work.

When reviewing Gabriela Mistral's *Selected Prose and Prose-Poems* for *Belletrista*, I said:

> Prose poems are interesting beasts. Formatted like prose, but with the compressed and heightened language of poetry, they live near the prose-poetry boundary, and sometimes have one foot on each side of that ill-policed border.[2]

And since prose poems are usually around the same size as small fictions, that blurring of boundaries is especially acute. The border is artificial, imposed by the diktats of publishing and marketing, with their requirements for everything to fit within a category – 'We regret to advise that your novel *Sexy Yet Gritty Modern Elves Who Ride Harleys* is too urban for the dark fantasy market and too dark for the urban fantasy market.' But at the same time, there are differences, the principal one being that short fiction is, like its longer cousins all the way up to the novel, concerned with narrative: in fiction, things need to happen. In poetry, things may happen, but that's not essential.

That said, much published New Zealand short fiction de-emphasises narrative in favour of the delineation of character development, and regards a moment of character growth – that fabled still, small epiphany – rather than the resolution of a major narrative question as the central payoff of fiction.

While I'll freely admit that many wonderful small fictions foreground character, my tendency is to prefer those that foreground narrative – and I believe that small fiction is a particularly good place to experiment with narrative.

One of the main complaints about experimental fiction is that it is hard to read. This is true almost by definition: if a work follows well-established storytelling tropes and uses comforting, familiar techniques, then it is not experimental, unless perhaps it is using those techniques only to subvert them. Although I enjoy reading experimental fiction, I find that it tends to pall the longer it becomes. The longer a narrative is, the more it needs the traditional architectures of fiction. Brevity circumvents this particular strain on the reader.

So what might these experiments with form consist of? Reviewing the excellent *The Best Small Fictions 2015* for *Beattie's Book Blog*, I noted these as my favourite stories in the anthology:

> But my personal favourites include 'A Notice from the Office of Reclamation', by J. Duncan Wiley, in which the institutional language of an official safety pronouncement battles human curiosity; the Northern-Ireland-set 'The Third Time My Father Tried to Kill Me', by James Claffey, with its time-reversed

> sequence of events; Lisa Marie Basile's 'Apocryphal'; 'Before She Was a Memory' by Emma Bolden, which has an opening line a scriptwriter would kill for; 'The Intended' by Dawn Raffel, a perfect cocktail of unease, expressed in striking imagery, which was my favourite story in this anthology; the single two-page-long paragraph of Julia Strayer's 'Let's Say'; and Ron Carlson's 'You Must Intercept the Blue Box Before it Gets to the City', which cunningly thwarted this reader's expectations of box-interception.[3]

Time-reversed narratives. A single, two-page paragraph (well, that's maybe not so experimental, but for all the efforts of José Saramago to popularise such things, it's still not common). A story told using the institutional language of an office safety pronouncement. And Ron Carlson's blue box story, which begins:

> Get that box! It must not get to the city; everybody knows that. It must be stopped from getting to the city. Go after the box and make sure it does not reach the city. Act quickly and intercept the box before it arrives in the city. Go to the shipping terminal and run through the big warehouse, past the conveyor belts carrying all the packages and boxes and cardboard tubes full of maps. Run![4]

and only gets stranger from there.

'Huh,' I hear someone say, 'call *that* experimental?' Which illustrates an important point: that what is considered 'experimental' depends on the reader making the determination, the time at which the determination is being made relative to the time the work was created, and the reader's own knowledge and preferences.

In 1913, when Stravinsky's 'Rite of Spring' received its première, it was considered so experimental, so avant-garde, so dissonant, as to be scandalous, and caused a near-riot in the audience. Now, over 100 years later, it is a respected and respectable warhorse of the concert repertoire – yet to ears that have only heard Bach and Mozart, it might still seem as outrageous as it did to that Paris audience on the night of 29 May 1913.

And thus it is in fiction too. Modernism, postmodernism: time and repetition dull the shock of the new.

If I had the job of handing out Great Writers of the Twentieth Century gongs, Jorge Luis Borges would be top of my list. Yet, in an era of novelistic inflation, Borges never published a work above twenty pages, and many of his works are extremely short, fitting comfortably into the category of small fictions. His greatness lay not in the delineation of character, but in his experiments with narrative time, narrative 'truth', and plot.

Borges's story 'Pierre Menard, Author of the Quixote' traces the unremitting efforts of the titular author to immerse himself so thoroughly in the works of the great Miguel de Cervantes that the imagined twentieth-century author Menard is able to recreate the seventeenth-century work, line by line, in its original Spanish. The narrator of the story notes how much greater an achievement this is than that of Cervantes:

> The Cervantes text and the Menard text are verbally identical, but the second is almost infinitely richer ... The contrast in styles is equally striking. The archaic style of Menard – who, in addition, is not a native speaker of the language in which he writes – is somewhat affected. Not so the style of his precursor, who embodies the Spanish of his time with complete naturalness.[5]

Many of Borges's small fictions play melancholy games with identity and time, none more so than 'Borges and I', which mournfully explores, in 350 words or so, the relationship between the self as person and the self as author:

> It's Borges, the other one, that things happen to. I walk through Buenos Aires and I pause – mechanically now, perhaps – to gaze at the arch of an entryway and its inner door; news of Borges reaches me by mail, or I see his name on a list of academics or in some biographical dictionary ... Years ago I tried to free myself from him, and I moved on from the mythologies of the slums and outskirts of the city to games with time and infinity, but those games belong to Borges now, and I shall have to think up other things.[6]

I don't always write small fictions – in fact, they tend to be what I turn to when I'm transitioning from a stint writing poetry to a stint writing fiction. But when I do write them, it's Borges I turn to for inspiration. An hour spent lost in his labyrinths sets the story ideas flowing.

But is my preference for experimental and narrative-driven fictions over mimetic and character-driven fictions a consequence of my gender?

When I interviewed her, *Best Small Fictions* series editor Tara L. Masih said:

> I find women are more willing in small fictions to tackle emotional subjects. Quite a few men whose work we've judged come at the form as more of an

exercise, an attempt to be clever or to play with the form in some way. Sometimes that works well and we've honored those stories, but often they don't hold up to, say, a story like 'Before She Was a Memory' by Emma Bolden, which continues to be recognized as a brilliant small fiction; it tackles the subject of a mother identifying her daughter at a morgue. Dark, but incredibly powerful. In under 1,000 words.[7]

I completely agree with Tara L. Masih that 'Before She Was a Memory' is one of the very best stories in *The Best Small Fictions 2015*, with its killer opening line:

> I didn't recognize her without her head.[8]

but as I noted above, it sits quite comfortably beside stories that are much more experimental in form, but no less affecting in content – at least to this reader – such as Julia Strayer's 'Let's Say':

> Let's say I'm being robbed, but I choose to believe I'm pushing my daughter on the swings in the park across from the Methodist church…[9]

The evidence of the two volumes of the *Best Small Fictions* series that I've seen suggests to me that women as well as men frequently play with form. It is possible to both play with form and tackle emotional subjects in the same story. Indeed, well-chosen experiments with form can enhance the emotional impact of powerful content.

The very brevity of small fictions generates a literary pocket universe in which there is room for the emotionally engaging alongside the intellectually engaging, the formally daring alongside the formally conservative, the ineffably poetic alongside the squarely prosaic. Room to explore the furthest reaches of both outer and inner space.

Small fictions can serve as confessional, laboratory, or both. There is no need for walls, and a lot of space for bridges.

---

1 S. Dybek and T. L. Masih (eds), *The Best Small Fictions 2016*, Queen's Ferry Press, Plano, TX, 2016.

2 T. Jones, 'Review: *Selected Prose and Prose-Poems* by Gabriela Mistral, translated from the Spanish by Stephen Tapscott', *Belletrista* no. 5 (2010), accessed from http://www.belletrista.com/2010/issue5/anth_4.php.

3 T. Jones, 'Review: *The Best Small Fictions 2015*', *Beattie's Book Blog* (2 February 2016), accessed from http://beattiesbookblog.blogspot.co.nz/2016/02/the-best-small-fictions-2015.html.

4 R.O. Butler and T. L. Masih (eds), *The Best Small Fictions 2015*, Queen's Ferry Press, Plano, TX, 2015, p. 109.

5 J. L. Borges, *Collected Fictions*, translated by Andrew Hurley, Penguin Books, London and New York, 1998, p. 94.

6 Ibid., p. 324.

7 'Feature Interview: Tim Jones talks with *Best Small Fictions* series editor Tara L. Masih', *Flash Frontier* (November 2016), accessed from http://www.flash-frontier.com/2016/11/19/november-2016-feature/.

8 Butler and Masih, *The Best Small Fictions 2015*, p. 56.

9 Ibid., p. 104.

Securing the empty spaces
Heather McQuillan

My great grandmother's marriage certificate bears two lies. In her wedding photo, 18-year-old Isabella Selina Barrette wears a hastily arranged lace collar over a tightly waisted linen jacket. On paper her age is given as 21 and her name as Isabel Barrett. Her parents knew nothing of her marriage to Fred Gooch, which took place in the parish church of Bromley St Leonards, London, on 9 November 1902. The tightly waisted jacket will not be worn for much longer.

At age 15, Isabella had trained as a milliner, but after her marriage, and the speedy arrival of their first child Margery, she and Fred took on the role of caretaker at The Rambler's Rest, a charitable organisation that offered a bed, a meal and a prayer for tramps, sailors, and anyone who needed it. It was there, in 1905, that my grandmother Elizabeth was born. During her life, and the ensuing wars, Bella raised six children and took on a number of cleaning and caretaking roles. Later in life, she managed market stalls in the east end of London and, of an evening, she made lace. According to stories passed down, petite Bella was never the delicate sort. Cheeky, robust, staunchly socialist, clever with making very short ends meet, yes, but neither frail nor dainty.

Needlework is one of the few things we New Zealand girls have as memories of our ancestry: treasured samplers from the early 1800s, an embroidered apron, lace doilies, each the craft of the girls and women from my mother's side, the delicate stitching of women who lived austere lives. Just as Bella wove a web of lies to make certain her marriage to Fred, the delicacy of her lacework is all illusion. Every cotton stitch is close, every hole in the pattern bound tight lest the whole work unravel. Bella's laceworks are the organisation of holes made sturdy by fine thread. My craft, flash fiction, is similarly small and full of holes yet, when it works, also tightly bound and anchored. And all lies.

That flash fiction is a like a lace tablecloth, using less thread than a tightly woven one yet covering the same surface area, was a glib answer I gave once to an interview question. It came to mind after I'd been contemplating how to repair a piece of my great grandmother's lace work that I had foolishly damaged with candle wax. It is an answer that I have enjoyed contemplating ever since – the role of flash fiction, not the removal of wax. A challenge implicit in writing flash fiction is that the hallmarks of what a reader expects of a story, such as character, setting, crisis and redress, need, by the brevity of words, to be merely suggested in the text, yet not so vaguely that the whole piece unravels and meaning is lost. Grant Faulkner says, 'The joy of flash fiction as a writer and a reader is found not only in the words of the story, but in what is left out – the absences can be almost spectral, haunting what's been told, only guessed at.'[1] This requirement for some 'guesswork' places a greater onus on readers to venture to traverse the spaces, but also a much greater responsibility on flash fiction writers to help them get there. The partnership between flash fiction writer and flash fiction reader relies on a great deal of trust from both sides. Working with few words to express expansive ideas, flash fiction writers have to ensure that the 'things unsaid', but essential to the telling, are tightly bound in the empty spaces, even though they are neither fully structured nor resolved. Spaces left too wide open to interpretation can swallow up or snag a reader. Such craft, like lacemaking, requires finesse, but do not equate this with daintiness. It is hard work, all this attention to detail: at times obsessive, grunty, sweaty attention to words.

Distilling a story into the very short form forces writers to scrutinise their word selections, not merely to fit within the specified word counts of journals and competitions, but, more importantly, to guide their reader to a coherent understanding of the text. Because a flash fiction writer cannot use all of the words available to her in order to make things explicit, individual key words must often play more than one role within the telling of the story. We are privileged, as explorers of the ways in which the poetic compression of language may also tell stories, to have a vast lexicon at our disposal. Out of the many words available to us will be ones to act as literary short-cuts, to create and combine etymological and social meanings, and to help us shape the sound, tone or stance of the piece we are writing. It is up to us, in the service of our readers, to challenge the quoted word of Samuel Taylor Coleridge, and lay claim that prose, as well as poetry, can be 'the best words in the best order'. In addition to the use of single key words to guide readers, we are able to yoke words, within and across sentences, to cue into readers' expectations and experiences. Our word choices become 'implications', pointing a reader towards unspoken sensations so that the text may become more that the sum of its parts. For example, the word lace (its etymology is from Latin *laqueus*, noose, and is akin to *lacere*, to entice or ensnare) brings its own connotations and assumptions within modern cultural contexts. Despite historical evidence that men designed, created and wore lace, it has become widely perceived as a feminine craft and fabric, and a 'womany' word.

As ladies wont, in pleasure's wanton lap, / To finger the fine needle and nyse thread
(Spenser, *The Faerie Queene, Volume 1*)[2]

When combined with other key words it may derive very different responses from readers.

Lace + wedding gown = fine, delicate, dainty, frail = chaste
Lace + spider web = mesh, entanglement, netted = entrapment
Lace + underwear = sheer, diaphanous, seductive = erotic

The use of even a seemingly simple word such as *lace* or *lacy* in a condensed piece of writing may summon forth myriad threads of connections to a reader's mind. The craft, and challenge, of the flash fiction writer is to pull these threads into patterns, to knot the words into strong images.

As in poetry, flash fiction forces the need for meticulous word choices, not only related to meaning, but also its sounds, its connotations, its evocations. Precision of word choice allows a reader to connect with the heft of the piece, to be able to see the patterns in the holes, to follow the twists, connections and insinuations that a longer piece of text might weave together more tightly. To extend the lace metaphor even further, flash fiction writers, like poets, are obligated to use words as precise, 'fine stitches', which in turn direct a reader's attention to the desired pattern. Even though a reader may miss certain stimuli offered, or project more on to the text than was ever intended, writers still hold an ethical responsibility in guiding a reader to coherence through the essential material available to them: words.

I have hated words and I have loved them, and I hope I have made them right.
(Markus Zusak, *The Book Thief*)[3]

So, how does a writer find the 'right' word? I can only speak of my own experience, so for what it's worth here is a glimpse of my processes. If I'm lucky, my 'automatic first draft writer' or subconscious throws up a surprising and perfect word that rather than being resisted or rejected deserves its place for reasons that may later, after due scrutiny, be self-evident. But more often I find myself in a struggle with key words that have ended up on the page but do not resonate with something I'm trying to do: maybe it's that the word adds nothing to the desired tone, or makes no contribution to a layer of desired meaning. Sometimes the 'automatic word', although it may appear as a perfectly suitable word in terms of its denotation, just doesn't resonate with the pattern of the story or with something in my head. I find myself holding a key word up to inspection, not only for its own merits but to see how it layers, collides, twists and knots with the other words already settled in the piece. A synonym may be selected because it adds strength to another word in another sentence; loops and pulls it tight, or perhaps it produces a sound that adds tonal qualities. More often than not I open up the thesaurus, and word after word is discarded until a single word slots into place like the last piece of the jigsaw. Regularly, it is the simplest and most precise word that is required, the simple stitch that ties off the ends neatly and prevents everything from unravelling.

Before her death in 1971, it was Bella's proud boast that she had outlived five monarchs, and had never called anyone 'Sir'. She waved goodbye to my family as we sailed off around the globe when I was only 18 months old and we never met again. I don't have memories of her. All I have is that wedding photo and a few pieces of lacework, some damaged by the careless use of a candle, cutwork with tight stitches, empty spaces secured by fine thread. And, perhaps, her tendency to weave lies.

---

1 Grant Faulkner quoted in Becky Tuch, 'Flash Fiction – what's it all about?' accessed 22 October 2017 from http://www.thereviewreview.net/publishing-tips/flash-fiction-whats-it-all-about.

2 Edmund Spenser, *The Faerie Queen, Volume 1*, J and R Tonson in the Strand, 1758, p. VIII.

3 Markus Zusak, *The Book Thief*, Picador, Sydney, 2005.

Segmentivity and the sequence: Prose poetry, flash fiction and hybrid forms

Airini Beautrais

Short forms such as poetry, prose poetry and flash fiction have an obvious feature in common: their division into distinct segments. In some cases, these segments are organised into sequences of various lengths. In addition to structural divisions, short forms can take different approaches to narrative: some tell coherent stories, some are primarily lyric, some essayistic, some descriptive, others anti-narrative, metafictional, or a combination.

In narrative media, the author can use segmentation in various ways: to assist interpretation, or to undermine it, or to offer a mixture of both. The interactions between the two variables of segmentation and narrativity (the degree to which a text is narrative) are likely to produce different effects in any given text.

The term 'segmentivity' was coined by poet and academic Rachel Blau DuPlessis in her 1996 essay 'Manifests'. Here, DuPlessis argues that it is the 'underlying characteristic of poetry as a genre', explaining: 'Poetry is the kind of writing that is articulated in sequenced, gapped lines and whose meanings are created by occurring in bounded units precisely chosen, units operating in relation to chosen pause or silence.'[1]

We can, of course, observe that poetry is not the only kind of writing, nor written language the only medium, in which bounded units are of significance. However, DuPlessis's term and its explanation provide a useful lens for considering poetry and other short forms. The relevance of DuPlessis's theory to the study of narrative in poetry was suggested by narrative theorist Brian McHale, who argues that 'segmentation *must always* contribute meaningfully (for better or worse) to the structure of poetic narrative'.[2]

New Zealand literature is studded with examples of sequential short forms: notable examples include Robin Hyde's *The Book of Nadath*, James K. Baxter's *Jerusalem Sonnets*, Anne Kennedy's *The Time of the Giants*, and Albert Wendt's *The Adventures of Vela*. As elsewhere in the world, the sequence is a form increasingly used in recent decades. These sequences include fiction, biography, autobiography, memoir and historical or political works. They range from short sequences within a longer collection to book-length works. Often these sequences are written as poetry. There are also recent examples of prose poem sequences or sequential flash fiction.

In this essay I consider two works by New Zealand writers, both published in 2016. One of these, Frankie McMillan's *My Mother and the Hungarians*, is a sequence of short short stories or flash fiction. The other, Simone Kaho's *Lucky Punch*, is a sequence of prose poems. I investigate how the variables of narrativity and segmentivity interact in each work, and I identify common threads.

One of the strategies available to a writer of sequential short forms, particularly where non-fictional genres such as history or autobiography are concerned, is that of selection and omission. A text made up of many small segments is likely to be less comprehensive than a text written in continuous prose, in which a reader would expect one chapter to flow logically on into the next. In non-fictional texts, this gives the writer the opportunity to leave out uncomfortable or uninteresting material. In all texts it allows for the undermining of narrative by reducing coherence and/or temporality. Both Kaho's and McMillan's works thrive on the significance of the gap. Neither tells a straightforward plot with beginning, middle and end. Both juxtapose past and present to create sudden temporal lurches. Both make use of segmentation to build stories made up of small, often disparate, kaleidoscopic pieces.

Lucky Punch moves between a child's-eye view and the perspective of a narrator looking back. These changes, along with changes in tense, are often quite abrupt, prompting readers to re-orient themselves at the beginning of each poem. Seven poems near the start of the sequence illustrate this. 'Waterview' is a present-tense descriptive poem about the narrator's childhood suburb, and what has changed there since the 1980s. The following three poems, 'Japanese Cedar', 'Fir Tree' and 'Oak' are all narrated in the past tense: the narrator reminisces about the garden of her childhood and the games she and her siblings played there. 'Spiders' begins: 'My sister is scared of spiders – has been ever since our neighbour threw a dead one at her.'[3] The temporal setting of this poem is uncertain. 'Sister' describes the relationship between the central character Henry and his sister. 'Wonder' is possibly from Henry's perspective and is narrated in the second person, present tense:

> Don't wonder how long until the nectarine falls, and if the chicken will get it, don't wonder if there'll be treasure in the garden, don't care about how it feels when you first feel her hands hit you and the push and pull – don't wonder if you'll do better this time and you'll be able to hurt her.[4]

These poems also demonstrate the interplay of narrative and lyric, which is continued throughout the text. *Lucky Punch* is described in its jacket copy as 'a love story set in tiny natural worlds': the natural worlds are certainly evident, as is a plot of sorts. There is a consistent narrator throughout, and other characters also maintain consistency, including the narrator's friend Henry, and various family members. The plot is based around the childhood friendship between Henry and the narrator, Henry's subsequent suicide, and the narrator's grief. Interestingly, the final poems trail off into other subjects. 'Over', the poem which makes Henry's death explicit (after others previously hinted at it), is followed by 'Jam', a poem about the narrator's father playing his guitar; 'Still', a poem about a flower, addressed to a 'you' figure who is probably Henry; and the final poem 'See', a short meditation on 'how people can feel different from how they look'.[5] Rather than operating in the familiar narrative mode of 'what happened next', these poems focus on emotional responses, showcasing the strong lyric impulse throughout this collection.

Some of Kaho's prose poems are stylistically straightforward paragraphs using traditional punctuation; others make use of sentence fragments and do away with punctuation. There are also a few lineated poems. 'Blues', narrated by a cameo character named Andy Blues, makes use of italicised speech and lineation to portray the disjunctive monologue of a drunk:

> *Do you want a cup of tea brother?*
> *How did we get home last night?*
> *Nah – good call good call.*
> *Things have moved on man*
> *it's another day.*
> *I'd give you that cat if it was mine*
> *I swear sister.*
> *Nah I'm Sāmoan, mainly Sāmoan.*[6]

Kaho's use of segmentation at the micro level reflects segmentation at the level of the poem: sometimes the flow is logical, sometimes it is disjointed; at all times the segments build collectively.

McMillan's *My Mother and the Hungarians* is mostly told through the eyes of a single narrator, a girl living in post-war Christchurch; however, there are multiple stories with other narrators. As with *Lucky Punch*, there are changes in chronology, and the tense switches between past and present. Characters are consistent: the girl narrator, her mother, her sister, her father, the eight Hungarian men who board at the family home following their arrival in New Zealand as refugees in the aftermath of the 1956 revolution. Perhaps the most interesting aspect of segmentation in this text is the insertion, in grey pages, of a section titled 'History is an alternating series of frying pans and fires', which is made up of seven poems relating to the Budapest uprising of October 1956. These poems feature several different narrators: a small boy, the sculptor Sándor Mikus who created the statue of Stalin, an unidentified man (possibly Mikus) who takes the statue's hand and buries it, and finally, the worms in the earth around the hand. Following this section, we are returned to Christchurch. Considered as a whole, the text contains no definite plot with beginning, middle and end. It certainly contains stories: each piece can be seen as a distinct flash fiction on its own. The events and effects of living with refugees are explored. Eventually, the Hungarians move on, and the narrator and her sister grow up and reflect on their childhood experiences. However, there is no climactic event, nor are there any clear goals, plans or desires on the part of the main narrator. The sequence does not progress towards any kind of teleological conclusion. Again, the interplay of narrative and lyric is important. The first half of the book contains a number of meditations on geography and orientation, with a recurrent theme of getting lost. The frequent disorientation of the narrator complements the stories of the refugees, divorced from their homeland and in a state of culture shock. While the second half of the book focuses solely on the Hungarian refugees and the girl whose home they live in, the first half deals more with the narrator as an adult, and is interspersed with seemingly unrelated poems featuring other characters and events. One such example is 'Falling in love the abseiler repeats the same tricky descent, over and over':

> Because he was an abseiler he was used to going back to what he knew and for that reason his first girlfriend was his only love. He thought he saw her in a picnic area by Hanging Rock. She sat on a rug, her red skirt ballooning in the breeze.[7]

Who is the abseiler, and who is his girlfriend? How does their story relate to the stories of the Hungarian refugees and the girl from Christchurch? As in *Lucky Punch*, there is the sense that ordering is at times thematic, and that each short piece is included for its mood or emotional significance as much as for its relevance to an underlying narrative. As well as giving the text lyrical qualities, the insertion of a variety of other stories complicates narrativity, and extends the possible interpretations of the text. Shifts in time, place, tense and narration create disturbances and dislocations which mirror the themes of the pieces themselves. The abrupt insertion of the middle section is almost violent: one history is catapulted into another. The occasional use of non-human perspectives, such as that of the worms in the soil, push the boundaries of realism. Incorporating these perspectives is a significant departure from the conventions of historical writing, shifting the focus from the factual representation of events to a creative re-imagining.

The approaches to chronology and geography seen in both texts suggest that the ordering of segments in a time sequence is very important to the interpretation of plot. As well as this, consistency of narration and character contribute to narrativity. Changes in tense, narration, time and place complicate narrative; the juxtaposition of different time periods or narrators, for instance, may temporarily disorient the reader, promoting a search for links or gap-filling.

Another point of consideration is the relative eventfulness of different texts, as well as the variations in eventfulness within a text. Both texts under analysis here contain events which would appear interesting, surprising or disturbing to the majority of readers: the 1956 Hungarian revolution; the fledgling romance between a Hungarian refugee and the narrator's mother; Henry's suicide. Both texts also make use of contrasts between eventful and uneventful material, such as Kaho's detailed studies of the 'tiny natural worlds' of Waterview. What has happened to the Hungarian refugees is eventful; a lot of what happens within *My Mother and the Hungarians* is relatively uneventful: going for bike rides, playing pin the tail on the donkey, conversations on the phone. Segmentation through the use of sequential short forms allows episodes of varying eventfulness to be placed alongside each other; to contrast the dramatic happenings of history and personal life with seemingly minor details which may, after all, turn out to be significant.

Both of these texts involve hybridity: poetic writing interspersed with prosaic writing, narrative interwoven with lyric. No doubt each also blurs the boundaries between fiction and non-fiction. Each offers welcome relief in its departure from literary norms. Sequential short forms appear to be particularly productive in expanding possibilities for hybridisation and the blurring of traditional genre distinctions. In these two examples, form is also intricately interwoven with content. Formal divisions are used effectively to portray the fragmentation of experience: historical events, childhood memories, and the nature of trauma and loss, amongst other things. As each of these texts demonstrates, the short-form sequence offers a broad range of possibilities, which can only be expanded upon by the continuing production of new work in this field.

---

1 Rachel Blau DuPlessis, 'Manifests', *Diacritics* 26, no. 3/4 (1996): 31–53, p. 51.

2 Brian McHale, 'Beginning to think about narrative in poetry', *Narrative* 17, no. 1 (2009): 11–27, p. 18.

3 Simone Kaho, *Lucky Punch*, Anahera Press, Auckland, 2016, p. 13.

4 Ibid, p. 15.

5 Ibid, p. 86.

6 Ibid, p. 25.

7 Frankie McMillan, *My Mother and the Hungarians*, CUP, Christchurch, 2016, p. 33.

The shadow-line, or: What's the difference between micro-fiction and prose poetry?

Jack Ross

Recently I attended a short story conference in Shanghai with a group of other New Zealand writers. Each of us was asked to give a reading. My wife Bronwyn Lloyd chose some short prose pieces from her forthcoming collection *A Slow Alphabet*, one of which used the recurring phrase 'the house didn't care' as a structural motif.

Afterwards, a young Chinese student questioned whether such a piece could actually be called a short story. In Chinese literature, she explained, there was a form called prose poetry, and she felt it might more properly fall under that heading. Bronwyn explained that we had the same genre distinction in English. I suppose what struck me most about the student's comment was the fact that she thought of this form as uniquely Chinese.

There's always been an air of the subversive about prose poetry in English. It's never been a form that vaunts itself: more like the poor cousin of 'true' poetry or 'real' prose. But what actually *is* the difference between a prose poem and a short short story (or micro-fiction, or flash, or any other term you prefer)? No doubt there are as many answers as there are writers, but that doesn't mean that no further distinctions are possible.

For instance, I tend to see the virtues of fiction of *any* length as including 'plot, characterisation, depth of immersion in "Mirror City" (to borrow Janet Frame's term for the world of her own writing).'[1] In prose poems, by contrast, I look for '[t]he sudden sparky connections, the topsy-turvy thinking: the need to read between the lines to be understood, which most of us would agree to be poetic virtues.'[2]

I remember clearly the strange and vertiginous effect some of Kafka's short parables had on me when I first read them as a teenager. One that particularly sticks in my mind is 'The Knock at the Manor Gate':[3]

> It was a hot summer's day. I was coming along the homeward road with my sister and passed the gate of a manor. I do not know if she knocked at it out of sheer mischief or merely threatened to do so with her fist and did not. A hundred yards farther up where the road turns left began a village. We were not acquainted with this village, but just after the first house people came out and waved at us. Whether out of friendliness or warning, they were apparently frightened and stooping in dismay. They pointed in

the direction of the manor we had passed and reminded us of the knock at the gate. The landlord had brought an action against us and an investigation was to begin at once. I was very calm and calmed my sister also. She probably hadn't even made any knock – and even had she done so, nowhere in the world was there proof of it. I tried to make the people around us understand. They listened, but withheld judgment. Later they said, not only my sister, but I too was to be charged. I nodded, smiling. We looked back at the manor, as when one observes a distant plume of smoke and waits for the flame. Dust rose, covering everyone. Only the points of the tall lances were visible. And scarcely had the troop vanished into the manor grounds when presently their horses appeared to have turned round, and were headed towards us. I pushed my sister aside – I would sort things out on my own. She refused to let me go by myself. I said she should at least change her clothes, so that she might come better-dressed before the gentlemen. In the end she followed and took the long way to the house. Soon the riders were upon us, nor had they alighted from their horses before they had asked for my sister. 'She's not here at the moment,' I answered anxiously, 'but she'll come later.' The answer was received quite indifferently; it seemed significant above all that they had found me. There were two main gentlemen: the judge, a young, lively man; and his quiet assistant who was named Assmann. I was asked to enter a peasant's cottage. Slowly, shaking my head and adjusting my braces, I sat down under the sharp gaze of the gentlemen at work. I still believed the word of honour, given by any of these peasants, would be enough for the townsfolk to set me free. But when I had crossed the threshold of the cottage, the judge, who sprang forward already expecting me, said: 'I feel sorry for this man.' However, it was beyond all doubt that by this he did not mean my present state of affairs, but rather what would happen to me. The room looked more like a prison-cell than a cottage: large flagstones, utterly bare walls, immured by an iron ring; something was in the middle – half platform, half operating table.

Could I still taste other air than the prison's? That is the great question; or on the contrary – it would be, if I still had some prospect of release.

It seems to me beyond question that this work of Kafka's constitutes a short short story, rather than a prose poem. But why is that? What is there about it that makes it seem like fiction rather than poetry?

For a start, there's its length. It's 530 words long (in translation: 499 in the original German). There's also a fair amount of characterisation: the brusque, rather pushy brother, who is determined to save his errant sister at all costs from the avenging 'gentlemen'. Then there's the sister herself, impulsive and volatile enough to knock (or gesture towards knocking) in the first place, but loyal enough to resist her brother's desire to take the whole blame on himself.

The 'young, lively' judge says only: 'I feel sorry for this man.' Then there's the chorus of avengers, 'the riders', as well as a chorus of villagers prophesying woe. The only person who *isn't* characterised clearly is the judge's 'quiet assistant', Assmann.

He is, nevertheless, the only named personage in the story. What's more, the fact that the judge is profoundly sorry for what is about to occur, and that the mention of that 'something' in the middle of the floor: 'half platform, half operating table', makes us fear the worst. Is Assmann a torturer? He's described simply as a 'quiet assistant' to the young judge, but there's a sinister implication behind that silence.

Kafka is at his best in short pieces such as this. The weight of implication in the two siblings' simple, almost non-existent act of transgression and the immense weight of authority expended on repressing it could hardly be more economically suggested. Far from an abandoned scrap, this short piece is in its own way as complete as any of his more famous stories: 'Metamorphosis', for instance, or even *The Trial* itself.

*

> The other night I was lying on a sofa … moaning and groaning and ingesting copious amounts of painkillers. A 'friend' decided to divert me by reading long passages from a book … called *Black November: The 1918 Influenza Epidemic in New Zealand* by Geoffrey W Rice. A nightmare and this prose poem were the inevitable results.[4]

For years I've been teaching the poem '1918' by poet and historian Scott Hamilton in my first year Creative Writing class:

> At the edge of Temuka the road is blocked by three bales of hay, a black flag, and the last two O'Shanessey kids, who take turns holding the rifle their cousin brought back from the Somme. Outsiders get sent back to the city; Maoris have to keep to Arowhenua, on the far side of the creek we dive in to wash the sickness away.
>
> When Queenie got the cramps we took her to the small house behind the marae, and laid her out on clean sheets, and fetched a bucket of creekwater, and cooled her stomach and hips, and washed the mushrooms under her arms. The younger kids giggled beside the bed, expecting another baby cousin. First her fingernails then her hands turned black; her breasts swelled, popped their nipples, and dribbled blue-black milk. We couldn't straighten her arms in the coffin, so we folded them across her chest. She looked like she was diving into herself.[5]

Why does Scott describe this as a prose poem rather than a short short story? Was it simply that, as a poet, he thought he should be writing poems? It was, after all, included in his first collection *To the Moon, In Seven Easy Steps* (2007). That book contains work in so great a variety of forms – essays, diary entries, left-margin justified poems – that it's hard to believe that Scott would feel constrained by any such conventions of nomenclature. I would prefer to argue, then, that this is *intrinsically* a prose poem – and not a mislabelled piece of micro-fiction. Why?

Certainly it lacks any of the play of character so obvious in the Kafka story. Its details are, if anything, even more horrific and disturbing, but Scott's piece makes much greater use of imagery and word-play.

> She looked like she was diving into herself.

This last sentence in Scott's evocation of the 1918 'flu epidemic sounds more like an observation than a thought. What does it *mean* to 'dive into yourself'? It is, I would suggest, a conflation of an attitude we associate both with intense introspection and with the finality of death.

The racist attitudes so apparent in the first paragraph of the piece – 'Maoris' this side of the stream, rifle-toting Europeans the other – are largely submerged by the brutal levelling effects of the disease itself, with its strange aping of childbirth and generation in its later stages.

But there's no real story here – in the sense of a forward-moving narrative. It would perhaps be possible to project one from the interaction of the 'last two O'Shanessey kids' – whether their siblings were killed in the war, or by the disease itself – and 'Queenie' down at the marae. But that would be our construction, not his.

His piece is universal in the sense that he means it to be extrapolated: the simple tragedy of death and fear it describes could be multiplied easily to cover the whole of New Zealand – and thence onto the rest of the world affected by the Spanish 'flu pandemic.

Kafka's piece, too, has its universal aspect: but in that case he wants us to take note of the incidents of the story: the initial act of disobedience, the terrifyingly disproportionate reaction to it. The manor, the village, the riders are all generic props by means of which he is able to impose this stark pattern on us. If they were more clearly delineated, it would detract from rather than enhance this intention.

Precisely the opposite is true of Scott's piece: specificity of place is necessary to give us the sense of multiple repetition he wishes to convey. The words 'many people died during the great pandemic' have little emotional resonance for us – and yet the fate of poor Queenie is hard to read, hard to endure, even through the medium of print. My students find it revolting – want to turn the page, even scribble over it – but once read, it's in their memories, and they can't escape it any more.

Mind you, it's true that Kafka's piece is more than three times as long as Hamilton's. Is this a more plausible explanation for the differences between them? Did the latter simply lack the space to sketch in more characters and flex his narrative muscles?

It's true that more space is generally required to animate a short short story than a poem. But I still feel that it's the differences in emphasis, the *genre* differences, between Kafka's and Hamilton's pieces, which are most significant: a poem is not simply a more condensed version of a short story, and neither is the most poetic piece of fiction a poem, exactly.

Perhaps, though, the virtue of all such works lies in their element of surprise – their ability to undermine our perception of an apparently static and ordered cosmos. The paradox inherent in their close resemblance to each other is simply another way of achieving this. It raises questions which might otherwise pass by unnoticed.

---

1 Jack Ross, 'Review of Frankie McMillan, *My Mother and the Hungarians and Other Small Fictions*', *Poetry New Zealand Yearbook 2017*, Massey University Press, Auckland, 2017, pp. 322–23.

2 Ibid.

3 Franz Kafka, 'The Knock at the Manor Gate', *Wikisource*, accessed 19 November 2016 from https://en.wikisource.org/wiki/Translation:The_Knock_at_the_Manor_Gate.

4 Scott Hamilton, '1918', *Reading the Maps*, accessed 19 November 2016 from http://readingthemaps.blogspot.co.nz/2006/03/1918.html. It should be noted that while the original title of the first edition of Geoffrey Rice's book was indeed *Black November: The 1918 Influenza Epidemic in New Zealand* (Allen & Unwin, Wellington, 1988), the second, revised edition, to which Scott is more probably referring here, was entitled *Black November: The 1918 Influenza Pandemic in New Zealand* (CUP, Christchurch, 2005).

5 Scott Hamilton, '1918', *To the Moon, In Seven Easy Steps*, Titus Books, Auckland, 2007, p. 99. This is the author's preferred text of the poem. It diverges slightly from the one recorded in his blogpost at http://readingthemaps.blogspot.co.nz/2006/03/1918.html.

Flash fiction – shaking the mixture
Martin Porter

At the start of the second millennium, poetry was the popular medium for passing verbal culture from place to place, generation to generation. It was not until the invention of the printing press, when books became simpler to produce and replicate in quantity, that the gulf between library and population could be more cheaply crossed. A new land of household prose was settled and the novel and textbook developed.

The fable, anecdote and novella sat somewhere between these two great genres, as do other more recently popular types of literature: prose poetry, short short story, micro-prose and flash fiction. These were like chains of islands, clearly defined above the waves but with rather less clear borders once the apparent surface is penetrated.[1, 2]

As technology has changed, so different genres of writing have gained visibility. Electronic media have allowed some forms to prosper, and even created new forms. The cost of production and propagation has reduced and so texting and microblogging (e.g. Twitter) have allowed new forms to grow.[3]

When writers explore the rifts between these genres, it can mean startling inventions. Initially unpromising circumstances lead to new forms. These new writing styles feed from the energy derived from pressurised and emergent environments. Seemingly toxic mixes sometimes produce creatures of strange and unexpected beauty. This is where exploration might be most exciting, albeit dangerous. The element of risk adds a frisson to this search for difference.

Flash fiction is well placed to make these explorations in an efficient manner. It sits close, perhaps overlaps, with many genres. It is relatively efficient to write. Experimenting by writing a novel is both risky and time-consuming, less so with flash. It has become easily available both in hard and electronic copy. It exists in anthologies, journals, blogs and even in the twittersphere. It is often free of charge. So for the reader, the time and money spent in taking the risk of reading an experimental work is reduced, and with it the likely sense of waste.

So where might exploration be fruitful? Breaking the linear story arc might be, perhaps using non-linear narration, parallelism and parataxis.[4] Non-narrative forms might also offer different approaches to telling a story. Much can be deduced from a simple shopping list, bill of items, inventory, pillow books or interview,[5] and filling in the gaps is one of the expectations of much flash fiction.

Flash fiction frequently relies on sleight of hand and ambiguity. Without this, flash can turn into little more than drafting or precis. In many ways, it offers readers an involvement that is often difficult to achieve in other longer form genres. Some flash expects active readers to take part in the process of authorship as much as the writer.[6]

Flash fiction shares much in common with other genres. It has the possibility of a story arc as found in narrative fiction, but also offers opportunity for language play. The structure and restrictions of language can be investigated by exploring the hinterland between flash and prose poetry. The use of assonance, metonymy, metaphor and allusion is common in flash, less common are lipograms, [7]reverse lipograms,[8] and n+7 restrictions.[9] Metafiction and self-reflexive fiction can open up the process of writing. [10, 11] The famous story 'Baby Shoes' attributed to Hemingway may itself be a meta-fiction.[12]

Flash fiction largely exists in the narrative tradition. This is practical. It conforms to modern story-telling conventions and so is accessible to both reader and writer. It fits well between prose and poetry. But to restrict it to just story-telling by narrow definition is dangerous. Flash fiction is 'fiction', not necessarily 'a fiction', an invention of the imagination, not just a truncated novel. While overindulgence is dangerous, austerity can be equally harmful. But, as Heraclitus warns, 'Where there is no strife there is decay. The mixture which is not shaken soon stagnates.'

---

1 C. Holdefer, 'How short is short?', *Journal of the Short Story in English*, 62 | Spring 2014, http://jsse.revues.org/1440

2 P. Casto, 'Flashes on the Meridian: Dazzled by Flash Fiction', http://www.writing-world.com/fiction/casto.shtml

3 B. Lucht, 'Flash fiction – Literary fast food or a metamodern (sub)genre with potential?', The 2nd Human and Social Sciences at the Common Conference, http://www.hassacc.com

4 Parataxis: a technique in which two images or fragments, usually starkly dissimilar images or fragments, are juxtaposed without a clear connection (https://en.wikipedia.org/wiki/Parataxis).

5 e.g. Sei Shonagon, *The Pillow Book*, ed. Meredith McKinney, Penguin, London, 2006.

6 e.g. as described in P. Trimarco and U. Hurley, 'Less is more: Completing narratives in miniature fiction', *Journal of Contemporary and Innovative Fiction*, 1(1), 2008, pp. 82–89.

7 Lipogram: a text that uses any and/or every letter of the alphabet with the exception of one (https://en.wikipedia.org/wiki/Lipogram).

8 Reverse lipogram: a text where each word must contain a particular letter (https://en.wikipedia.org/wiki/Reverse-lipogram). For an extended use of reverse lipogram, see Christian Bök, *Eunoia*, Coach House Books, Toronto, 2001.

9 n+7 restrictions: a text in which each of the substantive nouns is substituted by the noun appearing seven nouns away in a dictionary (https://en.wikipedia.org/wiki/Oulipo#Constraints).

10 Meta-fiction: a technique and a genre of fiction, wherein a fictional text is self-conscious or openly draws attention to the fact that it is imaginary (https://en.wikipedia.org/wiki/Metafiction). Self-reflexive: a technique and a genre of fiction where a fictional text reflects its own composition by responding to its own constructions (http://www.oxfordreference.com/view/10.1093/oi/authority.20110803100453429).

11 P. Casto, 'Flash Fiction: Brief and (Likely) Necessary Literature', private communication. (Originally published as http://abstractmagazinetv.com/2017/04/12/flash-fiction-brief-and-likely-necessary-literature-by-pamelyn-casto/)

12 D. Mikkelson, 'Ernest Hemingway – Baby Shoes', http://www.snopes.com/language/literary/babyshoes.asp

About the contributors

Alex Reece Abbott is widely published and anthologised. She has been featured in the Word Factory's 'Citizen' season, and her stories have won the Northern Crime, Arvon and Crediton prizes and been shortlisted for the Bridport, Tillie Olsen, Lorian Hemingway, HG Wells, Maria Edgeworth, Fish and Sunday Business Post/Penguin Ireland prizes. alexreeceabbott.info

Raewyn Alexander recently opened Zine Hope at Blue Haven Writing Workshops, Grey Lynn. She writes novels, poetry, stories, blogs, non-fiction, plays and reviews. She placed in *Landfall*'s Essay Competition 2011 and Printable Reality's Matariki Poetry Competition 2013. Recent works include *Glam Rock Boyfriends*, her 2016 poetry collection *Our Mother Flew Unassisted*, and a comic *Nothing and Nowhere (but Love)*. poeticjourneytoamerica.blogspot.co.nz/

Rosetta Allan is a novel writer with a history of poetry. Her debut novel, *Purgatory*, was published by Penguin Books in 2014. Rosetta is an active member of the New Zealand literary scene, and is currently working on her second novel.

Ivy Alvarez's latest collections are *The Everyday English Dictionary* and *Disturbance*. Her work is published widely, including in *Best Australian Poems*. She edits the New Zealand Poetry Society's magazine *a fine line* and, most recently, *Atlanta Review*'s New Zealand edition. Born in the Philippines and raised in Australia, she moved from Wales to New Zealand in 2014. ivyalvarez.com

Anita Arlov founded and MCs at Auckland's Inside Out Open Mic for Writers. She placed second in the Kevin Ireland Poetry Competition 2013 and was highly commended in the National Flash Fiction Day competition 2017. That same year she gained first place in the Divine Muses New Voices Emerging Poets Competition with 'Ballpoint'.

Sandra Arnold is an award-winning writer with a PhD in creative writing. She is the author of *Sing No Sad Songs*, *Tomorrow's Empire* and *A Distraction of Opposites*. Her short stories and flash fiction have been widely published and anthologised in New Zealand and internationally. Her work was nominated for the 2018 Pushcart Prize and the 2017 and 2018 *Best Small Fictions*. In 2019 her new novel *Ash* will be published by Mākaro Press (NZ) and her flash fiction collection *Soul Etchings* by Retreat West (UK).

Nick Ascroft was born in Oamaru to a teacher and a clergyman. Later, in Dunedin, he formed a band, MCd a weekly poetry reading and drifted into a career in publishing, which via Oxford and London has deposited him in Wellington, married and with a son. He has published three books of poetry and one on five-a-side soccer.

Lynn Tara Austin is very much into poetry. She began writing short poems which have grown a little in length. Now she has discovered flash fiction, these little works of art, she would love to write them too. Her piece in this collection, 'Meditation', is a haibun – prose plus haiku.

Sam Averis lives in Christchurch with his wife and daughters. He is an editor at *Flash Frontier*, and his stories have appeared in *takahē*, *Geometry*, *Psychopomp Magazine* and elsewhere. In 2016 two of his stories were highly commended in the National Flash Fiction Day competition. Find him online at samaveris.wordpress.com, and on Twitter @samaveris.

Tusiata Avia is a New Zealand-Samoan poet, performer and writer. She has published three books of poetry: *Wild Dogs Under My Skirt*, *Bloodclot* and *Fale Aitu/Spirit House* (which was a finalist in the 2017 Ockham New Zealand Book Awards), as well as a chapbook and two children's books. She has performed all over the world and held a number of writers' residencies and awards.

Hinemoana Baker is a New Zealand poet, musician, occasional broadcaster and creative writing teacher. She traces her mixed ancestry from several Māori tribes, as well as from England and Bavaria. Her latest collection of poetry is *waha | mouth* (VUP, 2014). She is currently living in Berlin, Germany, where she was the 2016 Creative New Zealand's Berlin Writer in Residence.

Sarah Jane Barnett is a poet, creative writing teacher and freelance editor. Her debut poetry collection *A Man Runs into a Woman* (Hue & Cry Press, 2012) was a finalist in the New Zealand Post Book Awards in 2013. Her second collection *WORK* was published in 2015. She is the literature editor for *The Pantograph Punch*.

Airini Beautrais lives in Whanganui. She writes poetry, fiction, essays and reviews. Her most recent collection is *Flow: Whanganui River Poems* (VUP, 2017).

Carrie Beckwith lives with her daughter, Grace, in Stratford upon Avon and is a Hagley Writers' Institute graduate. She's a frequent contributor to *Flash Frontier* and a nominee for the *Best of the Net 2017* anthology. She writes short stories and poems and recently completed NaNoWriMo, the ouput of which, her first novel, she's now editing. She runs Custom Content Ltd and helps businesses in New Zealand and the UK engage their audience with compelling online marketing.

Jenny Bornholdt has published ten books of poems, the most recent of which is *Selected Poems*. Her collection *The Rocky Shore* was made up of six long poems and won the Montana New Zealand Book Award for Poetry in 2009.

Nola Borrell's haiku and haibun have been published in New Zealand and overseas since the mid-1990s. Her publications include *waking echoes* (Korimako Press, 2013), a collection of haiku and haibun, and *this wide sky*, a chapbook (Puriri Press, 2012). Nola co-edited, with Karen P. Butterworth, *The Taste of Nashi*: *New Zealand Haiku* (Windrift, 2008).

Michael Botur lives in Whangarei and hails from Christchurch. He is a first-generation Kiwi of British, Irish and Polish descent. Michael is author of four short story collections and works in communications and journalism.

Liz Breslin's first poetry collection, *Alzheimer's and a Spoon* (OUP, 2017), made *The Listener*'s 100 best books of 2017. She's also an editor, columnist, playwright, MC and performer. Liz was second runner-up in the 2014 New Zealand Poetry Slam in Wellington, did a spoken-word piece and an audience-response poem at the 2016 TEDx Queenstown and came third in the Charles Causley Trust International Poetry Competition the same year.

Sarah Broom (1972–2013) completed her post-graduate study at Leeds and Oxford, held a post-doctoral fellowship at Massey University and lectured in English at the University of Otago. Her first book was *Contemporary British and Irish Poetry* (Palgrave Macmillan, 2006). Her first book of poetry was *Tigers at Awhitu* (AUP and Carcanet Press, 2010); her second collection, *Gleam*, was published posthumously (AUP, 2013).

Ben Brown is an award-winning children's author, poet and short story/non-fiction/freelance writer, with an occasional propensity toward performance poetry. He has performed throughout New Zealand and his work has been published around the world. Ben lives and works in Lyttelton.

Diane Brown is a novelist, memoirist and poet who runs Creative Writing Dunedin. Her publications include *Before The Divorce We Go To Disneyland*, *If The Tongue Fits*, *Eight Stages of Grace*, *Liars and Lovers*, *Learning to Lie Together* and *Here Comes Another Vital Moment*. Her latest book is *Taking My Mother to the Opera* (OUP, 2015).

Pete Carter has lived with his wife close to the bush near Wellington Harbour for twenty years. He has two collections of poetry and prose out and a children's book, *Our Dog Benji*, was published in 2017. One of his current projects is to see more of, and blog about, New Zealand. 'Starlings' was longlisted in the 2015 National Flash Fiction Day competition.

Janet Charman's collection 仁 *surrender* (OUP, 2017) responds to the perils and pleasures of her 2009 Hong Kong Baptist University writers' fellowship. Her discussion of the misogyny of Allen Curnow's introductions to his post-war poetry anthologies appears in 'A piece of why', *Poetry New Zealand Yearbook, 2017*.

Long ago, when theatrical aspirations collided with reality, **Stephen Charters** left London and returned home. Then, gradually, in the cracks between family, work and study, a slow accretion of small successes culminated in a creative writing degree. Now, while he subdues a steep section in a small northern town, an incomplete novel languishes.

Madeleine Child lives in Dunedin, hoping it will warm up. She has a couple of sons and a dog, and makes pots and art things. For the past couple of years she has been trying her hand at writing, and is surprised to find it not so very different from working with clay.

Joanna Cho is a writer from Auckland. She studied English at the University of Auckland and has been published in *Landfall*, as well as in various online publications.

Glenn Colquhoun is an award-winning poet and children's writer. His first collection, *The art of walking upright*, won the Jessie Mackay Best First Book of Poetry award at the 2000 Montana New Zealand Book Awards. *Playing God* (Steele Roberts, 2003), his third collection, won the Montana Poetry Award in 2003, plus the Readers' Choice Award. His essay collection is *Jumping ship and other essays*. His latest collection, *Late love – sometimes doctors need saving as much as their patients*, was published by BWB in 2016. He works as a GP in Horowhenua.

Carolyn Cossey has recently completed a Bachelor of Creative Writing at Manukau Institute of Technology. She has been published in *Flash Frontier*, *Headland* and *Landfall*. She is working on a historical novel based on the New Zealand huia. She lives in rural South Auckland with two teenagers and an assortment of horses, dogs and goats.

Celia Coyne's short stories and flash fiction have appeared in various journals, magazines and anthologies. When she moved from the UK to Christchurch, she fell in love with the sky. You can find more writing and photography on her website: mybeautifulsky.com.

Caroline Crick lives in Nelson. Her background includes farming, writing, photography and running a craft design studio. She looks forward to writing more fiction when time and work commitments allow. 'The man who kissed his wife' was shortlisted in the 2013 National Flash Fiction Day competition.

Mike Crowl is a writer, pianist and composer. Since 2012 he's written and composed a children's musical, and published four e-books: three fantasies for middle-grade readers and a non-fiction title. He blogs regularly, writes book reviews and poetry, and spends a lot of time accompanying local singers and instrumentalists in his home town of Dunedin.

Nikki Crutchley is a freelance proofreader and copy editor. She lives in Cambridge with her husband and two girls. Her flash has been published in *Flash Frontier*, *Mayhem Literary Journal* and the *Fresh Ink* anthology; two were shortlisted in the 2017 National Flash Fiction Day competition. Her crime/thriller *Nothing Bad Happens Here* was published in 2017.

Lilla Csorgo is originally from Canada. She is a produced playwright, has had the odd short story published and is struggling to get her novels noticed. You can find out more about her and her work at www.lilla.ca.

Makyla Curtis is Scots Pākehā. She recently completed an MA in English at the University of Auckland and is currently studying te reo Māori. Makyla was awarded the 2017 Ema Saikō Fellowship at the New Zealand Pacific Studio. She is a letterpress printer, poet and printmaker. makyla.wordpress.com

Morgan Davie's fiction has been published in journals such as *JAAM*, *Enamel* and *TSV*. He also writes for digital games, tabletop games and immersive experiences. His blog, about story, interactivity and where they cross over, can be found at taleturn.com.

Melanie Dixon is a writer of flash fiction, short stories, creative non-fiction, poetry and novels for children. Her work has been published and anthologised internationally. She is a graduate of Hagley Writers' Institute and a tutor at the School for Young Writers.

Allan Drew recently completed his PhD in creative writing at Victoria University of Wellington. He writes mostly fiction, but also poems and non-fiction. His work has been published in journals and anthologies in New Zealand, the UK and the US. Allan teaches creative writing and science writing at Massey University.

Sarah Dunn is a journalist who graduated from Victoria University with a BA Hons in English literature and religious studies. Sarah spent time in Korea on an Asia New Zealand Foundation internship and placed first in the 2014 National Flash Fiction Day competition.

Lynley Edmeades's poetry, essays, reviews and scholarship have been published widely in New Zealand, Europe, Australia and the US. Her debut book of poetry, *As the Verb Tenses*, was published in 2016 by Otago University Press.

Annette Edwards-Hill lives on the south coast of Wellington. She completed the Victoria University poetry workshop in 1997 but swapped poetry for flash fiction in 2013. She was longlisted for the National Flash Fiction Day competition in 2017 and was winner of the *Flash Frontier* 2017 Winter Writing Award.

Anne Else is a Wellington writer and editor. Her published work has focused mainly on New Zealand women, history and social change. Her first personal book, *The Colour of Food: A memoir of life, love & dinner* (Awa Press, 2014), was a finalist for both the Food Writers Culinary Book Quill and the Bert Roth Labour History Award.

Michelle Elvy edits at *Flash Frontier* and *Blue Five Notebook*. She is assistant editor of *The Best Small Fictions* series and was an associate editor of *Flash Fiction International*. Recent work appears in *New Micro Fiction* (W.W. Norton, 2018), *Manifesto: A Political Anthology* (OUP, 2017), *Borderlands and Crossroads: Writing the Motherland* (Demeter Press, 2017) and *To Carry Her Home* (Bath Flash Fiction, Volume One, 2016). michelleelvy.com

Tracy Farr lives in Wellington and is the author of two novels, *The Life and Loves of Lena Gaunt* and *The Hope Fault*. Her short fiction has won awards, including the 2014 *Sunday Star-Times* Short Story Award, appeared in literary journals, magazines and anthologies, and (along with her first novel) been broadcast on Radio New Zealand. 'Beer goggles' was highly commended in the 2012 National Flash Fiction Day competition. tracyfarrauthor.com. Twitter: @hissingswan

Fiona Farrell publishes poetry, fiction, non-fiction and plays. Her first novel, *The Skinny Louie Book*, won the New Zealand Book Award for fiction in 1993 and since then she has been regularly shortlisted, uniquely among New Zealand writers, in fiction, poetry and non-fiction. Other awards include the Menton Fellowship, the Prime

Minister's Award for Literary Achievement (Fiction) and the New Zealand Order of Merit for services to literature (2012).

Rachel J. Fenton lives in Auckland. Her work can be found in *First fox* (The Emma Press), *Island to Island* (UpStart Press), *Rialto*, *The Lonely Crowd*, *Flash Frontier* and *Landfall*. In 2016 she was runner-up in the Ambit Summer Competition, and received funding from Creative New Zealand for a graphic biography of Mary Taylor, Charlotte Brontë's best friend.

Joan Fleming is the author of two poetry collections published by Victoria University Press, *The Same as Yes* (2011) and *Failed Love Poems* (2015), and a chapbook, *Two Dreams in Which Things are Taken* (Duets, 2010). Her honours include the Biggs Poetry Prize, the Verge Prize for Poetry and the Harri Jones Memorial Prize from the Hunter Writers Centre.

Anna Forsyth is a New Zealand-born poet, fiction writer and editor currently living in Newcastle, NSW. Her work has appeared in *Landfall*, *Poetry New Zealand*, *FourW* and the *Canberra Times*, among other publications. She is the founder and convener of the feminist poetry event series, Girls on Key.

Janis Freegard's most recent publications are a novel, *The Year of Falling* (Mākaro Press, 2015), and a poetry collection, *The Glass Rooster* (AUP, 2015). Born in the UK, she grew up in South Africa, Australia and New Zealand. She is a past winner of the Katherine Mansfield Award, lives in Wellington and blogs occasionally at janisfreegard.com. 'Elephant' was runner-up in the 2012 National Flash Fiction Day competition.

Nod Ghosh lives in Christchurch. Her work can be found in *Love on the Road 2015* (Liberties Press), *Horizons2* (NZSA, 2015), *Leaving the Red Zone* (Clerestory Press, 2016), *Landmarks* (UK NFFD, 2015) and *Sleep is a Beautiful Colour* (UK NFFD, 2017), and various online and print journals. 'Shape shifters on the bus' won second prize in the 2016 National Flash Fiction Day competition. nodghosh.com

Céline Gibson has been published nationally and internationally. She graduated from Hagley Writers' Institute in 2014. Her collaboratively written screenplay 'Unit 9' won the 2016 Moondance International Film Festival, and her stage play 'Stitched Up' was performed in Christchurch in 2015 by CAS'n'OVA Productions. Céline's favourite short story form is flash fiction.

Robyn Gosset was educated at St Margaret's College and the University of Canterbury where she obtained an MSc (Hons) in zoology and was a Sir George Grey Scholar. She has been a freelance journalist for sixty years, has written seven non-fiction books and has work in several anthologies. She is also a book reviewer.

Anna Granger lives by the Whanganui River. Her short stories have won awards and prizes, been published in magazines and collections, and broadcast on radio. As well as writing, she works with ARAN Animal Rescue NZ, the pound-dog rescue trust she founded in 2007. Her story 'Territories' won the 2014 BNZ Short Short Story Award.

Paula Green is a poet, blogger, anthologist, reviewer and children's author with an Italian doctorate. In 2017 she received the Prime

Minister's Award for Literary Achievement – Poetry and was made a Member of the New Zealand Order of Merit for services to poetry and literature. She runs NZ Poetry Shelf (nzpoetryshelf.com), and her latest book is *Wild Honey: Reading New Zealand women's poetry* (OUP, 2018).

Bernadette Hall lives in a renovated bach at Amberley Beach in North Canterbury. Her most recent books are *Life & Customs* (VUP, 2013) and *Maukatere, floating mountain* (Seraph Press, 2016). In 2015 she received the Prime Minister's Award for Literary Achievement – Poetry, and in 2017 was made a Member of the New Zealand Order of Merit for services to literature.

Trisha Hanifin writes short stories, flash fiction and creative non-fiction, and has recently completed a novel, *Ghost Travellers*. Her work has been published in *Fresh Ink*, a 2017 anthology of New Zealand writing, *Ingenio*, *Turbine*, *Flash Frontier*, *Headland* and *To Carry Her Home* (Bath Flash Fiction, Volume One, 2016). 'With our eyes closed we begin to dance' won second prize in the 2014 National Flash Fiction Day competition.

Michael Harlow has published eleven books of poetry, most recently *Nothing For It But To Sing*, which won the Kathleen Grattan Poetry Award in 2015 and was published by Otago University Press in 2016. 'The moon in a bowl of water' was commended in the 2016 National Flash Fiction Day competition.

Siobhan Harvey's books include *Lost Relatives* (Steele Roberts, 2011), *Cloudboy* (OUP, 2014) and *Essential New Zealand Poems* (Random House, 2014). Lecturer at The Centre for Creative Writing, AUT, she won the Kathleen Grattan Poetry Award in 2013 and holds a 'Poet's Page' on The Poetry Archive (UK).

Dinah Hawken is a poet who lives in Paekakariki on the Kapiti Coast. Her seventh collection of poetry, *Ocean and Stone*, was published by Victoria University Press in 2015.

Helen Heath's debut collection of poetry, *Graft*, won the Jessie McKay award for Best First Book of Poetry in the New Zealand Post Book Awards in 2013 and was the first book of fiction or poetry to be shortlisted for the Royal Society of New Zealand Science Book Prize. Her new collection of poems is called *Are Friends Electric?* (VUP, 2018).

Sally Houtman (1962–2017) was an American-born writer who made her home in Wellington with her children, Johannes and Anneke. She wrote her first flash in 2012 and was nominated that year for a Pushcart Prize and highly commended in the National Flash Fiction Day competition. Sally cherished her friends in the writing community and her work was published in New Zealand and abroad.

David Howard spent thirty-five years writing *The Incomplete Poems* (Cold Hub Press, 2011) and a further six completing *The Ones Who Keep Quiet* (OUP, 2017). He is the editor of *A Place To Go On From: The Collected Poems of Iain Lonie* (OUP, 2015).

Gail Ingram writes poetry and short stories. Her flash fiction has been placed in international competitions, and in 2016 she won the New Zealand Poetry Society's

International Competition. She has been a finalist for *The Best Small Fictions*, shortlisted for the Fish Short Story Prize and nominated for the Pushcart Prize. She holds a Masters of Creative Writing from Massey University. 'Dragonfly collage' was commended in the 2016 National Flash Fiction Day competition.

Rata Ingram writes poetry, essays and short stories from the foot of Christchurch's Port Hills. Her work appears in *The Perch* (Yale, 2017) and *after the cyclone* (NZPS, 2017). She was a featured reader at National Flash Fiction Day in 2016 and 2017. Rata is currently the vice president and youngest member of the South Island Writers' Association.

Kamala Jackson was awarded a first class Master of Creative Writing from AUT in 2010 for *Freedom Struggles*, a first draft novel. Her work was longlisted in the 2016 National Flash Fiction Day competition. *Emory*, a book written jointly with friends, was self-published in 2017. She is still working on her novel.

Teoti Jardine is Māori, Irish and Scottish. His tribal affiliations are Waitaha, Kāti Mamoe and Kāi Tahu. He attended the Hagley Writers' School. His work has appeared in the Christchurch *Press*, *London Grip*, *Te Karaka*, *Ora Nui*, *Catalyst*, *JAAM* and *Flash Frontier*; he guest edited, with Vaughan Rapatahana, the 2018 Pasifika edition of *Flash Frontier*. He and his dog Amie live in a beautiful old house in Linwood, Christchurch, New Zealand.

Jac Jenkins generally lives a quiet rural life writing poetry and flash fiction. She has spent the last two years as an explorer of capability – living for nine months of 2016 in the Northern Territory of Australia, and then participating in Victoria University of Wellington's 2017 MA in creative writing where her writing extended into creative non-fiction. 'The possum hunt' was highly commended in the 2012 National Flash Fiction Day competition.

Lynn Jenner's first book, *Dear Sweet Harry*, won the Adam Foundation Prize in Creative Writing as an MA thesis and then the NZSA Jessie MacKay Best First Book of Poetry prize in 2010. Her second book, *Lost and Gone Away*, was shortlisted for the Ockham New Zealand Book Awards non-fiction category in 2016. See pinklight.nz for more about Lynn's work.

Elysia Rose Jenson is a short story writer and aspiring novelist from Christchurch. Her short fiction has been published in literary journals, anthologies and magazines in both New Zealand and the UK. She lives with her wife in London.

D. R. Jones writes flash fiction, epigrams and novels. His work has been published in *Landfall* and *Flash Frontier* and was commended in National Flash Fiction Day 2017.

Tim Jones was awarded the NZSA Janet Frame Memorial Award for Literature in 2010. His books include his second short story collection *Transported* (Vintage, 2008), poetry anthology *The Stars Like Sand: Australian Speculative Poetry*, co-edited with P. S. Cottier (Interactive Press, 2014), and his fourth poetry collection *New Sea Land* (Submarine imprint, Mākaro Press, 2016).

Brindi Joy has lived in Seattle, Denver and New Orleans; she currently lives in Christchurch, where she makes the most of the mountains and the sea. She has been an organiser for National Flash Fiction Day in Christchurch since 2014. Her fiction and non-fiction have been published nationally and internationally. 'Secondhand palm' was longlisted in the 2013 National Flash Fiction Day competition.

Simone Kaho is a graduate of the International Institute of Modern Letters in Wellington. Noted for her powerful stage presence, she performs regularly at writers' festivals, theatres and live music venues, often with musicians. Simone's first book, *Lucky Punch* (Anahera Press, 2016), was launched in 2016 to warm reviews ('Utterly compelling' – Anne Kennedy) in *Metro*, *The Herald*, *Pantograph Punch* and *Landfall*.

Rosalie Kempthorne is an ordinary office worker by day, and the ruler of multiple universes by night. She sometimes wonders if she should consider getting more sleep.

Erik Kennedy is the author of the chapbook *Twenty-Six Factitions* (Cold Hub Press, 2017), and his first full-length book of poems is *There's No Place Like the Internet in Springtime* (VUP, 2018). He is the poetry editor for *Queen Mob's Teahouse*. Originally from New Jersey, he lives in Christchurch.

Sue Kingham writes short stories, poetry, flash fiction and creative non-fiction. Her writing can be found in *Flash Frontier* and *takahē*. In 2014 she placed third in both the National Flash Fiction Day and National Poetry Day competitions. Sue lives in Christchurch, but many of her stories are inspired by her English roots or her travels.

Lynne Kohen is a writing student living in Ruby Bay, Nelson. Her poetry awards include second and third placements in the New Zealand Poetry Society's International Poetry Competition, and first equal in the Page and Blackmore Annual Poetry Contest. 'Salt' was commended in the 2016 National Flash Fiction Day competition.

Saradha Koirala is a Nepali/Pākehā writer from Wellington. She is the author of poetry collections, *Wit of the Staircase* (Steele Roberts, 2009) and *Tear Water Tea* (Steele Roberts, 2013), and the young adult novel, *Lonesome When You Go* (Mākaro Press, 2016), which was the 2017 Storylines Notable Book Award Winner – Young Adult Books. Saradha currently works as a secondary school teacher in Melbourne.

Koenraad Kuiper's poetry has been published in New Zealand, Canada and the Netherlands. In New Zealand his poems have appeared in *Islands*, *Landfall*, *Poetry New Zealand*, *Sport* and *takahē*. He has published four books of poetry at ten-year intervals: *Signs of Life*, *Mikrokosmos*, *Timepieces* and *Bounty*.

Graeme Lay was born in Foxton and grew up in coastal Taranaki, where he learned to love the sea. He is a graduate of Victoria University of Wellington. He has published fiction for adults and young adults and collections of short stories and travel writing. Much of his work is inspired by the islands of the South Pacific. He works from his home in Devonport, Auckland.

Wes Lee lives in Wellington. Her latest collection, *Body, Remember*, was launched in 2017 by Eyewear Publishing in London. Her poems have appeared in *Westerly*, *Poetry London*, *Poetry New Zealand*, *New Writing Scotland* and many other publications. Her writing awards include the BNZ Katherine Mansfield Literary Award and the Saboteur Awards Best Anthology 2017.

Michele Leggott was the inaugural New Zealand Poet Laureate (2007–09) and received the Prime Minister's Award for Literary Achievement – Poetry in 2013. Her collections include *Vanishing Points* (2017), *Heartland* (2014) and *Mirabile Dictu* (2009), all from Auckland University Press. She coordinates the New Zealand Electronic Poetry Centre (nzepc) with Brian Flaherty at the University of Auckland.

Fiona Lincoln writes legislation by day and stories by night. Her flash fiction has appeared in *Flash Frontier* and *The Lobsters Run Free* (Bath Flash Fiction, Volume Two, 2017).

Kate Mahony has an MA in creative writing from the International Institute of Modern Letters, Victoria University. Her fiction has been published in numerous literary magazines and has placed in international competitions. Her work appears in various print anthologies, including *The Best New Zealand Fiction 6* (Random House, 2009), *Landmarks* (UK NFFD, 2015) and the *Fish Anthology* (Ireland, 2015). katemahonywriter.com

Catherine Mair is a writer from Katikati in the Bay of Plenty. Her short short stories have appeared in the Tandem Press anthologies, 1997 to 2005, as well as *takahē* and *A Bridge Above Water* (New Fiction, UK, 2001). Catherine enjoys speeding around Katikati's haiku pathway on her e-trike, but she can't race her athletic granddaughter in an up-hill sprint.

Bill Manhire lives in Wellington, and is best known for his poetry and short fiction. Over the last few years he has also been writing song lyrics for the musicians Norman Meehan and Hannah Griffin.

S. J. Mannion is an Irish writer living in Christchurch. She writes, widely and variously, poetry, flash fiction and creative non-fiction. She also writes collaboratively and commercially with other artists. She is published in New Zealand, Ireland, the UK and the US.

Selina Tusitala Marsh is a Pasifika poet-scholar and the current New Zealand Poet Laureate (2017–19). As the 2016 Commonwealth Poet she wrote and performed a poem for the Queen at Westminster Abbey. She has three critically acclaimed collections of poetry and lives in hope that one day, maybe one day, her sons will write her a poem. She is poetically married to David and is also a Waiheke Islander.

Owen Marshall has written or edited thirty books. Awards include the Montana New Zealand Book Awards Deutz Medal for Fiction, the 2013 Prime Minister's Award for Literary Achievement – Fiction, Officer of the New Zealand Order of Merit and Companion of the New Zealand Order of Merit for services to literature. He is an adjunct professor at the University of Canterbury, which awarded him the honorary degree of Doctor of Letters.

Stephanie Mayne is an Auckland librarian. Her poetry has been published in newspapers, anthologies and online literary journals.

Mary McCallum is an award-winning novelist and poet who has turned to publishing, establishing Mākaro Press in Wellington in 2013. She placed third in the 2013 National Flash Fiction Day competition and judged the 2014 competition. 'Dead Space' won third prize in the 2013 National Flash Fiction Day competition.

Allan McEvoy has spent most of his working life dealing with challenging behaviours and risk in the role of a frontline mental-health social worker. He now divides his time between writing, teaching, gardening and generally participating, with the knowledge that each of these activities will improve the world. 'Leader of the pack' was runner-up in the 2016 *North & South* Short, Short Story competition.

Timothy McGiven is a property rights analyst who writes short stories in his spare time. He recently graduated with his Masters from the University of Waikato and now lives in Wellington with his wife Hannah and cat Tilly. 'Crack' was shortlisted in the 2012 National Flash Fiction Day competition.

Himali McInnes works as a family doctor in South Auckland – a place rich with stories and many small kindnesses. She is also a beekeeper, a part-time vet and a constant gardener. She enjoys writing flash fiction, short stories and travel articles.

Leslie McKay, formerly of Christchurch and Sydney, is now a West Coast poet/writing tutor. In 2016 she won the Caselberg Trust International Poetry Prize. In a collaboration with Lisa Tui Jonathan, a number of her poems have become songs.

Frankie McMillan's latest book, *My Mother and the Hungarians, and other small fictions* (CUP, 2016), was longlisted for the Ockham New Zealand Book Awards. She was the Writer in Residence at the University of Canterbury in 2014, and at the Michael King Centre/ University of Auckland in 2017. Frankie is a contributor to *Flash Fiction International* (W. W. Norton, 2015) and *The Best Small Fictions 2017* (Braddock Avenue Press). In 2018 she was a *Best Small Fictions* finalist.

Heather McQuillan is director of The School for Young Writers in Christchurch. She won the National Flash Fiction Day and Micro Madness competitions in 2016 and was a Pushcart Prize nominee in 2015. Recent stories appear in the anthologies *The Best Small Fictions 2017* (Braddock Avenue Books), *Sleep is a Beautiful Colour* (UK NFFD, 2017) and *The Lobsters Run Free* (Bath Flash Fiction, Volume Two, 2017).

Zoë Meager has a Master of Creative Writing from the University of Auckland and her short stories have been commended and published at home and abroad. There's more about her work at zoemeager.com, and Twitter @ZoeMeager. 'A mother's touch' was winner of the 2016 *North & South* Short, Short Story competition.

Courtney Sina Meredith is a poet, playwright, fiction writer and musician. Her award-winning play *Rushing Dolls* (2010) was published by Playmarket in 2012. She launched her first book of poetry, *Brown Girls in Bright Red Lipstick* (Beatnik), at the Frankfurt Book Fair 2012, and has since published a short story collection, *Tail of the Taniwha* (2016), to critical acclaim.

Vivienne Merrill was a finalist in the 2017 Micro Madness competition and has had her work published in *Flash Frontier*. Writing as Vivienne Joseph, she is an award-winning author of stories, poetry and children's books. Vivienne also works as a freelance editor on the series *Children of the Pacific*, and on other projects.

Eileen Merriman's young adult novels include *Pieces of You* (Penguin, 2017) and *Catch Me When You Fall* (Penguin, 2018). Awards include a 2018 Storylines Notable Book Award for *Pieces of You*, third place (three times) in the 2014–2016 *Sunday Star-Times* Short Story competitions, second in the 2015 Bath Flash Fiction Award and first in the 2016 Graeme Lay Short Story Award.

Louise Miller has been writing short fiction for many years and is a contributor to *Flash Frontier*. She currently lives and works in rural Otago. 'Indian summer' was highly commended in the 2015 National Flash Fiction Day competition.

Harvey Molloy's most recent book is *Udon by The Remarkables* (Hoopla Series, Mākaro Press). His poetry has appeared in numerous journals in New Zealand and overseas. His first book of poems was *Moonshot* (Steele Roberts, 2008). He is also the co-author, with Latika Vasil, of the book *Asperger Syndrome, Adolescence, and Identity: Looking Beyond the Label.*

Elizabeth Morton is an Auckland scribbler. She is included in *The Best Small Fictions 2016*, and came second, twice, in the *Sunday Star-Times* Short Story competition. She is feature poet in *Poetry New Zealand Yearbook 2017*. Her first poetry collection, *Wolf*, was published in Mākaro Press's Hoopla Series in 2017.

Linda Moser is an aspiring soul mate, mother, teacher and, occasionally, writer. Her work includes flash fiction, short stories, travel writing and two novels. Linda has had some success, in all areas of her writing, both nationally and internationally. 'The wheat field' won third prize in the 2016 National Flash Fiction Day competition.

Emma Neale writes poetry and fiction and works as an editor. Her most recent novel, *Billy Bird* (2016), was shortlisted for the Acorn Prize in the 2017 Ockham New Zealand Book Awards and was longlisted in the International Dublin Literary Awards.

Piet Nieuwland wrote conservation strategies for Department of Conservation Te Papa Atawhai in Northland after training as a forester. His poems and flash appear in *Landfall*, *Brief*, *Catalyst*, *Poetry New Zealand*, *Pure Slush*, *Otoliths*, *Cordite*, *Mattoid*, *Blue Five Notebook*, *Atlanta Review* and elsewhere. He edits *Fast Fibres Poetry* and reviews poetry for *Landfall.*

Poet, editor and writer for children, **James Norcliffe** has published nine collections of poetry, including *Shadow Play* (Proverse, 2013) and *Dark Days at the Oxygen Café* (VUP, 2016). He is editor at *Flash Frontier*, former poetry editor for *takahē*, and a leading light in the Canterbury Poets' Collective.

Heidi North has been published in New Zealand, Australia and the UK. She won an Irish poetry competition in 2007, and has won awards for short fiction. She was the New Zealand fellow on the Shanghai International Writers Program in 2016. In 2017, she received the Hachette mentorship to work on her first novel. Her debut poetry book is called *Possibility of Flight*.

Keith Nunes lives beside Lake Rotoma where the two of them undertake a great deal of reflecting. He's been published around the globe, placed in competitions and is a Pushcart Prize nominee. His book of poetry/short fiction is *catching a ride on a paradox*.

Gregory O'Brien is a Wellington-based writer and artist. Recent books include a collection of poems, *Whale Years*, and a book about New Zealand photography for young people, *See What I Can See* (both AUP, 2015). A collection of essays exploring the relationship between art and the environment, *Always song in the water*, is in the pipeline.

Rachel O'Neill is a filmmaker, writer and artist based in Te Whanganui-a-Tara. Her debut book, *One Human in Height*, was published by Hue & Cry Press in 2013.

Maris O'Rourke enjoys performing and producing, and likes to have many projects on the go at once. She has been published nationally and internationally, and has published a poetry collection, an e-book family history and four children's books – the latter in English and Māori. 'Three firsts' was the winner of the Printable Reality/New Zealand Poetry Society Matariki Poetry competition 2013.

Eileen Palmer was born and raised in Dumfries, Scotland, the land of Robert Burns. She lives with her husband, two wonderful teenagers, six chickens, three alpacas and one fat cat in North Canterbury. Writing creatively is an outlet for her wild imagination, which is constricted by her accounting day job.

Janet Pates lives in the North Waikato township of Tuakau and is a writer of fiction and fact for both children and adults. Her writing reflects her background of teaching and farming, and her interest in local history. Her children's novel *Mystery At Tui Bay* won the Tom Fitzgibbon Award. She admires the minimalist qualities of flash fiction. 'Last ride' was the winner of the 2012 National Flash Fiction Day competition.

Kiri Piahana-Wong is of Māori (Ngāti Ranginui), Chinese and Pākehā (English) ancestry and lives in Central Auckland. She is a poet and editor, and the publisher at Anahera Press. Her poems have appeared in many journals and anthologies, and she has edited editions of *JAAM* and *Flash Frontier*. Her first poetry collection, *Night Swimming*, was released in 2013.

Patrick Pink has been writing short stories and flash fiction for years and has been published nationally and internationally. His stories have been nominated for a Pushcart Prize and the *Best of the Net 2017* anthology.

Patrick was the recipient of the first place prize in the National Flash Fiction Day 2017 competition.

Vivienne Plumb is of New Zealand and Australian heritage, and is based in Aro Valley, Wellington. She has published nineteen books of poetry, short and long fiction, drama and non-fiction. She is the recipient of the 2017/18 Creative New Zealand Berlin Writer's Residency. Her new collection, *As Much Gold as an Ass Could Carry*, was published by splitfountain, Auckland, in 2017.

Martin Porter, born in Jersey, studied astrophysics in London and Leeds. He now lives in Whangarei, where he writes poetry and micro-prose. His flash fiction has been published in *Storm Cellar*, *Bare Fiction*, *Blue Five Notebook* and *Flash Frontier*. He is twice winner and occasional judge of the Whangarei Libraries Flash Fiction competition.

Joanna Preston is a Tasmanaut poet, editor and freelance creative writing tutor. She lives in semi-rural Canterbury with a flock of spoilt chooks and an overgrown garden.

Chris Price is the author of three poetry collections, including *Beside Herself* (2016) and the genre-bending 'biographical dictionary' *Brief Lives*, all published by Auckland University Press. She has also contributed to the art-science anthologies *Are Angels OK?* (2006) and *Transit of Venus |Venus Transit* (2016). Chris teaches creative writing at Victoria University of Wellington.

Patricia Prime is co-editor of *Kokako*, reviews/interviews editor of *Haibun Today* and a reviewer for *Atlas Poetica*, *takahē* and other journals. She also writes poetry and articles. She co-edited, with Dr Bruce Ross, *100 Tanka by 100 Poets* and *The World Haiku Anthology: A Vast Sky*, and has published a collection of haibun and tanka sequences, called *Shizuku.*

Leanne Radojkovich's début collection of stories is *First fox* (The Emma Press, 2017). Her work was translated into Chinese for the 14th International Conference on the Short Story in English, held in Shanghai, where she co-presented 'The "V" Word – Voice in the NZ Short Story', and her flash fiction street art has popped up around the world. 'First fox' won second prize in the 2015 National Flash Fiction Day competition.

Maggie Rainey-Smith is a novelist, poet, short story writer, essayist and book reviewer. The Greek translation of her third novel, *Daughters of Messene*, a New Zealand bestseller, is due for release in 2018.

Vaughan Rapatahana lives in Aotearoa New Zealand, the Philippines and Hong Kong, and is published internationally across several genres. In 2016 he won the inaugural Proverse Poetry Prize and his poetry collection, *Atonement*, was nominated for a national book award in the Philippines. His latest collection is *ternion* (erbacce-press, Liverpool, 2017). In 2018 he guest edited, with Teoti Jardine, the Pasifika edition of *Flash Frontier*.

Harry Ricketts has published around thirty books, including collections of poems, literary biographies, personal and critical essays, and several anthologies. He is a professor of English at Victoria University of Wellington, where he teaches English literature and creative writing. Folly House, a mock-Venetian pile on Folly Bridge in Oxford, really exists. Harry Ricketts lived there, 1973–74.

Jack Ross is the managing editor of *Poetry New Zealand*, and works as a senior lecturer in creative writing at Massey University's Auckland campus. His latest book, *The Annotated Tree Worship*, was published by Paper Table Novellas in late 2017. He blogs at mairangibay.blogspot.com/.

Nina Seja is a writer, curator and academic. She is widely published in both fiction and non-fiction. She was awarded her PhD from New York University and is a senior lecturer in communication studies.

Kay Shacklock has come to writing late in life, but not too late. An Auckland-based pianist, she has written two family musicals, 'Stout Heart' and 'Patch', produced by Howick Children's and Youth Theatre in 2015 and 2017, respectively. Kay has also had musically-themed short stories published in several overseas anthologies.

Kerrin P. Sharpe has published four collections of poetry: *Three Days in a Wishing Well* (2012), *There's a Medical Name for This* (2014), *Rabbit Rabbit* (2016) and *Louder* (2018), all from Victoria University Press. Her poems have been published in a wide range of journals in New Zealand and internationally, including *Oxford Poets 13* (Carcanet Press, UK) and *Poetry* (Chicago).

Tina Shaw is the author of several novels, including *The Children's Pond*, and her short stories have been widely published. She has held the Creative New Zealand Berlin Writers' Residency, and was the 2005 Writer in Residence at the University of Waikato. She is a creative writing tutor and book reviewer.

Emma Shi recently completed her studies in classics at Victoria University of Wellington. She was the winner of the National Schools Poetry Award 2013 and the Poetry New Zealand Prize 2017, and runner up in the *North & South* Short, Short Story competition in 2015. Her work has been published in literary journals such as *Landfall* and *Flash Frontier*.

Cherllisha Silva lives and writes poetry and prose in Pukerua Bay, Wellington. Her work is published in *NZPS Anthology*, *Plate in the Mirror* (Printable Reality), the *School Journal* (NZ) and the *School Magazine* (Australia). In 2012 she shared the R. G. Frean Prize for creative writing at Massey University. She is currently studying at the International Institute of Modern Letters, Victoria University.

Rebecca Simons thinks there's no better way to sharpen her skills than to work with a word limit. She won *Flash Frontier*'s 2013 Summer Writing Award and was also nominated for the Pushcart Prize for one of her flashes in the same year. Some of her longer works can be found on *Wilderness House Literary Review*.

Tracey Slaughter's latest collection of short fiction, *deleted scenes for lovers* (VUP), was longlisted for the Ockham New Zealand Book Awards 2017. She was the 2015 winner of the *Landfall* Essay Prize and the 2014 winner of the international

Bridport Prize. She teaches at Waikato University, where she edits the literary journal *Mayhem*. In 2018 she judged, with Sue Wootton, the National Flash Fiction Day competition.

Madeleine Slavick has authored several books of photography, poetry and non-fiction: *Fifty Stories Fifty Images*, *Delicate Access*, *Something Beautiful Might Happen* and *Round – Poems and Photographs of Asia*. She has exhibited her photography internationally and across New Zealand (Aratoi Museum, Victoria University, Wallace Arts Centre). She came to New Zealand from Hong Kong, where she lived for 25 years, and where 'Skyscraper, moon, sea' is set.

D. F. Smale is fascinated by the ways people internalise the world around them and how they express what they see. D. F.'s hobbies include scrapbooking, macramé and ignoring trivial problems until they become insurmountable issues.

Rachel Smith's poetry and fiction have been published in print and online journals in New Zealand and overseas. She placed second in the National Flash Fiction Day 2017 competition. Rachel is the fiction editor for *takahē*, judge for Micro Madness and script writer for the feature film 'Stranded Pearl' (2018). Rachel's website is rachelmsmithnz.wixsite.com/rachel-smith and she tweets at @rachelmsmithnz1. 'The window is closed' was commended in the 2016 National Flash Fiction Day competition.

Vivienne R. Smith has had poetry and prose published in *takahē*, *Blackmail Press*, *Deep South*, *Junctures*, *Turbine* and *4th Floor*. She holds an MA in creative writing (2013) from the International Institute of Modern Letters, Victoria University of Wellington. A scientist by training, and a public servant by necessity, but her heart and mind both expand when she writes.

Elizabeth Smither is a poet, novelist and short story writer. She was named the Te Mata Poet Laureate in 2002 and made a Member of the New Zealand Order of Merit for services to poetry and literature in 2004. Her prizes include the New Zealand Book Award for Poetry (1990), the Montana New Zealand Book Award for Poetry (2000), the Prime Minister's Award for Literary Achievement – Poetry (2008) and the Sarah Broom Prize for Poetry (2016). Her latest collection of poems is *Night Horse* (AUP, 2017), which won the 2018 Ockham New Zealand Book Award for Poetry.

Grant Stone's stories have appeared in *Island*, *Shimmer*, *Strange Horizons* and *Semaphore*, and have twice won the Sir Julius Vogel Award. His novella, *The Last*, is available from Paper Road Press.

M. B. Stoneman lives in an old BNZ bank in Patea, South Taranaki. She is an exhibiting printmaker and works for the local district council coordinating arts projects in seven rural towns. In 2017 she released two books, *The Nun & The Poet: Jerusalem* (self-published) and *The Menagerie – An Alphabet Book* (Little Wing).

Barbara Strang is a poet and editor who was born in Invercargill and now lives at Mt Pleasant, Christchurch. Her published work includes the poetry collections *Duck*

Weather and *The Corrosion Zone*. She has a special interest in Japanese forms: haiku, tanka and haibun.

Kirsten Strom is a young writer, composer and conductor. Born in New Zealand, she spent much of her childhood overseas but ended up in the same little West Auckland house her parents built. She conducts school and community ensembles and her pieces have been played by national orchestras. Her writing captures the everyday moments that make up our lives.

Rebecca Styles has completed a PhD in creative writing at Massey University where she wrote a novel based on an ancestor's experience of mental illness at Seacliff Asylum. Her short stories have been published in New Zealand journals and anthologies. She teaches short story writing at Wellington High School Community College. 'Parade' won second prize in the 2013 National Flash Fiction Day competition.

Jane Swan lives in Waikouaiti, Dunedin. Her work appears in *The Best Small Fictions 2015*, *Flash Frontier* and other online magazines, and has been broadcast on RNZ National and placed in several writing competitions. She is fond of the members of her writing group, Waitaki Writers.

Mere Taito is originally from the island of Rotuma. She emigrated from Fiji to New Zealand in 2007. Her work has appeared in New Zealand and international literary publications such as *Landfall*, *Manifesto Aotearoa* and *So Many Islands* (Commonwealth Writers, London). She lives in Hamilton with her partner, Neil, and nephew, Lapuke.

Jeff Taylor is retired and living in Hamilton. He is winner of the 2015 New Zealand Writers College competition and two UK short story competitions (Global Short Stories), and placed second in the 2014 BNZ Short Short Story Award. He was awarded the 2016 *Flash Frontier* Summer Writing Award.

Vivian Thonger, born in London, is a writer, poet and performer now based in Kerikeri. Her flash fiction and poetry appear in *Offshoots 13+14*, writeupnorth.co.nz, *Flash Frontier* and *International Flash Fiction*. 'Sick day' was awarded Northland Short Story of the Year 2017. She performs at events and festivals with Northland's Poetry Posse and ImprovMob.

Emma Timpany was born in Dunedin and grew up on the Otago Peninsula. Previous publications include *Over The Dam* and *The Lost of Syros*, and she is co-editor of *Cornish Short Stories: A Collection of Contemporary Cornish Writing* (The History Press, 2018). Her short stories have won three awards and been published in New Zealand, Australia and England.

Reuben Todd is a writer and comic. *The Poet Creep* (2017) is his first book. 'Miri' was longlisted in the 2014 National Flash Fiction Day competition.

Tim Upperton's second poetry collection, *The Night We Ate The Baby* (Haunui Press, 2014), was an Ockham New Zealand Book Awards finalist in 2016. His poems are anthologised in *The Best of Best New*

Zealand Poems (VUP, 2011), *Villanelles* (Everyman, 2012), *Essential New Zealand Poems* (Random House, 2014) and *Obsession: Sestinas in the Twenty-First Century* (Dartmouth University Press, 2014).

Kathryn van Beek is a graduate of Victoria University's International Institute of Modern Letters. Her short stories have appeared in *Headland*, *Hue and Cry*, *Pot Roast* and *Aerodrome*, and she won the 2015 Headland Prize. Kathryn has also written and illustrated a children's book, *Bruce Finds A Home*, based on the adventures of her infamous internet cat.

Latika Vasil lives in Wellington. Her stories have been published in various anthologies and journals and broadcast on Radio New Zealand. Her collection of short stories, *Rising to the Surface*, was published in 2013 by Steele Roberts and she is currently working on a new collection of interlinked stories.

Richard von Sturmer was born in Devonport in 1957. His published works include *We Xerox Your Zebras* (Modern House, 1988), *A Network of Dissolving Threads* (AUP, 1991), *Suchness: Zen Poetry and Prose* (HeadworX, 2005), *On the Eve of Never Departing* (Titus Books, 2009), *Book of Equanimity Verses* (Puriri Press, 2013) and *This Explains Everything* (Atuanui Press, 2016).

Ann Webber is an Australian and 'trailing spouse' currently living in Worcestershire, England. She wrote 'Peacock' while living in New Zealand and a member of the Auckland-based International Writers' Workshop. Ann says writing provides a permanent space in which to feel at home while constantly moving. Her stories often reflect themes of belonging. 'Peacock' was runner-up in the 2012 National Flash Fiction Day competition.

Elizabeth Welsh is a poet, short fiction writer and academic editor from Auckland. She is currently working on her first poetry collection.

Tom Weston's most recent collection of poetry, *What is Left Behind* (Steele Roberts, 2017), was longlisted for the 2018 Ockham New Zealand Book Awards. His work has appeared in various journals and anthologies, including the online series *Best New Zealand Poems*.

Keith Westwater's debut poetry collection, *Tongues of Ash* (IP, 2011), received the 2011 IP Picks Best First Book prize. Other publications include *Felt Intensity* (2015) and *No One Home* (2018), both from Mākaro Press. His work has appeared in *Landfall*, *JAAM*, *Snorkel* and *Idiom 23*, and has received or been shortlisted for awards in New Zealand, Australia and Ireland.

Brendon Stanton White lives in Christchurch. His work has been published in *Headland*, *Flash Frontier* and *Flash Fiction Magazine*. He won the Macmillan Brown Prize for Writers in 2015.

Sian Williams is a writer and editor. Her flash fiction has been successful in competitions in New Zealand and internationally. From 2012 to 2014 she was an editor at *Flash Frontier*. Sian lives in Kerikeri, writing fiction and growing kiwifruit. 'Ophelia at Huntly' was the Northland regional winner in the 2016 National Flash Fiction Day competition.

Nicholas Williamson lives in Christchurch. He has published two books of poetry, *The Whole Forest* (Sudden Valley Press, 2001) and *The Blue Outboard* (Black Doris Press, 2016), and a picture book, *The Curious Story of Harris and His Near Death Experience* (Yacob and Tomas, 2016).

Iona Winter (Waitaha/Kāi Tahu) lives in Waitati, Dunedin. Her fiction has been anthologised with *Bath Flash Fiction*, *Nottingham Peacebuilders*, *Halo*, *Elbow Room* and *Ora Nui*, and has also appeared in *Flash Frontier*, *Reflex Fiction* and *The Island Review*. In 2018 Iona was shortlisted for the Bath Novella-in-Flash Award. Passionate about Aotearoa, Iona writes hybrid forms that highlight the intersection between written and spoken word.

Sue Wootton lives in Dunedin. Her most recent publications are her debut novel *Strip* (Mākaro Press, 2016), which was longlisted for the fiction prize in the 2017 Ockham New Zealand Book Awards, and her fifth collection of poetry, *The Yield* (OUP, 2017), which was shortlisted for the 2018 Ockham New Zealand Book Awards. Sue co-edits *Corpus: Conversations about Medicine and Life* (corpus.nz). In 2018 she judged, with Tracey Slaughter, the National Flash Fiction Day competition. Sue's website is suewootton.com. 'Calligraphy' was highly commended in the 2016 National Flash Fiction Day competition.

Phoebe Wright is a writer and English teacher based alternately in Christchurch and in Gulu, Northern Uganda. In 2017 she attended the Hagley Writers' Institute, working on poetry, flash fiction and a novel. Her writing projects are increasingly inspired by her time in Uganda, exploring themes of globalisation, neo-colonialism and feminism in the developing world.

Louise Wrightson has an MA (Distinction), Creative Writing, from the International Institute of Modern Letters, Victoria University of Wellington. She lives and writes near Otari-Wilton's Bush, a 100-hectare reserve of regenerating forest. Her book, *Otari: Poems & Prose*, was published by Otari Press in 2014.